COPING WITH ABUSE
IN THE FAMILY

CHRISTIAN CARE BOOKS

Wayne E. Oates, Editor

COPING WITH ABUSE
IN THE FAMILY

by

Wesley R. Monfalcone

THE WESTMINSTER PRESS
Philadelphia

Scripture quotations from the Revised Standard Version
of the Bible are copyrighted 1946, 1952, © 1971, 1973
by the Division of Christian Education of the National
Council of the Churches of Christ in the U.S.A., and are
used by permission.

Book Design by Dorothy Alden Smith

First edition

Published by The Westminster Press®
Philadelphia, Pennsylvania

PRINTED IN THE UNITED STATES OF AMERICA
9 8 7 6 5 4 3 2 1

LIBRARY OF CONGRESS CATALOGING IN PUBLICATION DATA

Monfalcone, Wesley R   1942–
    Coping with abuse in the family.

    (Christian care books ; 10)
    Bibliography: p.
    1. Family violence — United States. 2. Problem
family — United States. 3. Family — Religious life.
4. Family social work — United States. 5. Helping
behavior. I. Title. II. Title: Abuse in the family.
III. Series.
HQ809.3.U5M66   362.8'2   80-15125
ISBN 0-664-24326-6

To
My family by birth
and
My family by choice

For nurture, joy, and love

Contents

Preface

Every family is plagued with abuse. It may be mild and subtle abuse that keeps us from realizing dreams of love and fulfillment. It may be more serious abuse that drains energy, cripples parents and children, and constricts life. It may be serious, violent, even fatal abuse.

This book is written to three audiences. Persons who are involved in subtle abuse may find here confrontation and a call to repentance. It is only as you and I admit our sin, see its destructiveness, and seek the forgiveness of family members and of God that we can be reconciled and healed.

Those involved in more serious forms of abuse that lead to emotional and spiritual crippling, and sometimes to physical disability and death, will find here understanding and guidance. A great deal has been discovered about child abuse, spouse abuse, and self-abuse (especially suicide), but the persons caught in these tangled webs rarely have access to that knowledge. You need to know that there are persons who understand and care, and that there are many who want to help.

The potential helper is the third audience. There are many persons sensitive enough and courageous enough to see subtle and serious abuse occurring in families around them. They want to help but find it difficult to "get a handle" on these problems. The professional or layperson who wants to help is obligated to get in touch with his or her own pattern of abuse in relationships. Chapters on the subtle abuses are presented first as a way of providing common ground for understanding and action. Only when you and I have faced the log in our own eye can we help our brother or sister remove their speck (or log). As we get in touch with that part of ourselves which yields to temptations to abuse, we can help with another's burden without hypocrisy or condemnation.

The first chapter addresses the apparent contradiction in terms of this book. How can we talk about abuse occurring in a family that is genuinely Christian? Some concepts are introduced that interpret abusive behavior and a Christian approach to the problem.

The chapter on subtle abuse includes us all. In sharing this information on several occasions with a variety of audiences, I have always seen smiles of recognition and nodding of heads. Each group, in fact, has been able to come up with several more categories to add to the list of subtle abuses from their own family relationships.

Religious abuse in families, and abuse of families by organized religion, is widespread and difficult to confront. How does one question a parent, sibling, or pastor who feels that it is of ultimate importance to behave in a certain manner because God requires or expects it? It is easy to observe abuses in other families and other churches, but we are not so quick to detect them in our own.

Part I includes us all. Part II is for those who are tangled in severe abuse, and for those who would help them.

Child abuse is a widespread, yet hidden, problem. In spite of its existence in families of every creed, color, and economic level, child abuse is usually hidden away in closets of shame and embarrassment. The isolated nature of these families increases the strain and makes reaching them difficult. My hope is that this book will be placed in the hands of abusive parents and will communicate some understanding of the struggles, along with genuine assurance that help is available and change is possible.

I have similar hopes for persons enmeshed in spouse abuse. No matter which one is the victim or the victimizer, a couple caught up in abuse need generous doses of understanding, care, and loving confrontation. Help is available.

The last chapter focuses on an underlying assumption of the whole book: every form of abuse of other persons has an element of self-abuse. To hurt those closest to us is to limit our own possibilities for giving and receiving love and security. Suicide is the ultimate form of self-abusive behavior.

As you read these pages, my hope is that you will be confronted with your own abusive behavior and with a challenge to change and to help others to change. You and I are assured that we can do all things—however impossible they seem—through him who strengthens us (Phil. 4:13).

Acknowledgments

I want to express my deep gratitude to those who have been particularly helpful in writing this book:

Wayne E. Oates, who invited my participation in this series, and who has been a helpful editor and guide in writing.

Carol Morse, Director of the Spouse Abuse Center in Louisville, Kentucky, who reviewed and made helpful suggestions on the spouse abuse chapter.

Madeline Reno, Director of Project FIND, a child abuse prevention and treatment service in Louisville, Kentucky, who reviewed and made suggestions about the child abuse chapter.

Rebecca, my wife, who reviewed the manuscript and had many helpful suggestions.

Catherine Shands, my secretary, who labored through the roughest of rough drafts.

Susan Hilker and Tish Gardner of Southern Baptist Seminary Office Services, for the typing of the final draft.

Persons who have shared their lives with me as their pastor, chaplain, or counselor, and who have taught me the dynamics of family abuse and family forgiveness.

PART
I
FOR SUBTLE FAMILY ABUSERS
(You and Me)

1. Use and Abuse

Abuse? In the *Christian* family? You've got to be kidding!

No, family abuse is no kidding matter. Abuse does happen in the Christian family. The whole scale from subtle, socially acceptable neglect to extremely violent mistreatment happens in Christian families.

UNDERSTANDING ABUSE

The basic meaning of "to abuse" is to use improperly, to misuse, to treat another person with harshness born of insensitivity or of malicious intent. Look at the Family Abuse Scale on page 19. We may think of abuse as ranging from socially acceptable ignoring, through verbal and physical mistreatment, to physical violence. All of us at some time in our development are involved in family abuse.

There is a *proper use* of family members. We use husbands, wives, children, and other relatives to meet normal healthy needs. God has planned that "for this cause shall a man leave father and mother and cleave to his wife, and the two shall become one." In the beauty of committed marriage two persons can satisfy their needs for love, companionship, sexual fulfillment, and security. The children of that home can enjoy security, trust, and steady growth to maturity in an atmosphere of committed love.

But in seeking to meet our own needs, we can misuse others. We can and sometimes do become overly demanding and manipulative when we feel that our well-being or even our survival is threatened. We may feel pushed by internal and external stresses to injure even those we care for most.

How can this be in the Christian family? Doesn't being Christian make us different from others who do not experience the grace of God and the fellowship of the church?

Yes, it does make a difference. All things are become new in Christ. We are redeemed sinners—but we are sinners yet. Some of the most evil—and most foolish—behavior we can observe occurs when religious people believe themselves to be so sanctified that they can do no wrong. Convinced they are led by the Holy Spirit, they think anything they do is certainly the work of God in them. You and I, truly redeemed by the work of Jesus, may come to feel ourselves utterly pure, perfect, and free from sin. But to be human is always to fall short of the glory of God. The writer of Hebrews said that our Lord experienced every temptation common to man, "yet without sin." We experience every temptation common to persons, but the "yet without sin" phrase cannot be added about us. To be human is to be less than God, less than perfect, and in need of confession and repentance.

We often think of the New Testament era as being the "ideal" time of the Christian church, the period when things were as they ought to be. A close look shows that the early church had its share of abuses. Acts 6 records the story of the Greek widows who felt they were being short-changed in the distribution of goods; the result was the selection of a group who were probably the first deacons. Ananias and Sapphira were caught in deception (Acts 5). Peter had diffi-

FAMILY ABUSE SCALE

	IGNORING	WITHDRAWAL	BERATING	PHYSICAL NEGLECT	VIOLENCE	HOMICIDE/SUICIDE
MINIMUM Consequences	Loss of Intimacy	Loss of Intimacy Loss of Companionship Loss of Parental Modeling	Loss of Self-Esteem	Loss of Affection	Injury Feelings of Shame and Guilt	Death Prison Mental Hospital
MAXIMUM Consequences	Divorce Movement up the scale	Divorce Acting out Movement up the scale	Runaway (children/teens) Divorce Mental Illness Movement up the scale	Sickness Divorce Movement up the scale	Injury Death Divorce	Death Prison Mental Hospital

culty overcoming his prejudices against Gentiles (Gal. 2:11). Paul wrote to exhort the churches as they succumbed to temptations—including factional bickering, prostitution, incest, slander, and gossip (I Cor. 5:1; II Cor. 12).

One of the strengths of the New Testament is that the humanness of the early Christians shines through. These were no plastic saints who had been zotted into perfection. They were people like you and me who had to struggle with all manner of temptations, without and within, and they found that they had to rely on the grace and forgiveness of God rather than on their own good works.

The present church is not so different from the first-century church in this regard. The sensitive pastor in a new church picks up many clues to unhappy persons in abusive relationships among the members. The pastor becomes aware of a woman whose husband spends all of the family's money on alcohol and gambling, of a man whose wife stopped functioning as a wife after their baby was born, of a child whose parents constantly berate or beat him. The pastor who gets to know members of the fellowship deeply will see many signs of withholding, manipulation, neglect, and physical violence among family members.

How can it be that Christians may abuse those persons who are closest, who mean the most? The answer is in the question—we misuse them because they are so significant. Not only are they the handiest objects for our frustration, we may feel intense anger when they are "failing" us. What are some specific conditions that breed abuse?

Controlled by the Shadow

A concept I find very helpful is the idea of the "Shadow Self." We all have a public self that we are willing and eager to show others. Usually these are the socially acceptable traits—good humor, respect for authority, affection, trust, good deeds, good thoughts, good feelings. We also have a very private self the Shadow Self which we rarely expose to the light. This may include anger, sexual desires, laziness, greed; in short, all manner of attitudes and feelings that are not acceptable to persons who are important to us.

Christians are often reared in homes and churches that discourage open expression and encourage repression of some thoughts, feelings, and behavior. We may learn early that anger is not to be openly expressed, that sexual thoughts and feelings are not permitted, that in order to be considered "good" persons we must ignore significant aspects of our humanity. Our chief aim in life is to be rid of these dark spots.

But there are disadvantages to hiding the Shadow Self. Keeping significant segments of ourselves repressed requires a good deal of energy. We may become robotlike, unable to express any feelings, because of the great energy expended to submerge all feelings. Another disadvantage: it simply does not work! Powerful parts of ourselves that are submerged will eventually leak out. A husband angry with his wife but unable to express that anger may become quite a "joker," and his humor has such a sarcastic hack that the humor is more destructive than open anger. When we are not in touch with the Shadow Self, we find that, as Paul says, "I do not understand my own actions. For I do not do what I want, but I do the very thing I hate" (Rom. 7:15).

Living Out Scripts

Another influence on family abuse, and another way of looking at the Shadow Self, is to see how we live out our life scripts. This concept of transactional analysis is easy to understand. All of us get messages from parents, brothers and sisters, teachers, pastors, friends, about who we are and what kind of life we will live. Many times I have heard it said of preschoolers: "Johnny's our thinker"; "Susan is going to be a nurse"; "Charles will make a preacher someday." Other messages are communicated either subtly or bluntly: "You're going to turn out just like your Uncle Marvin" (the millionaire); "You're acting just like your Aunt Josephine" (the family black sheep); "You remind me of Cousin Ralph" (now in the state penitentiary).

Each of us carries these messages around with us. They play a significant part in the drama of our lives. Subtly and often without conscious awareness we decide: "Yes, I am like Uncle Fred who messed up his life and committed suicide at thirty-four"; "Yes, I am like Aunt Margaret who was left with six children to raise after her husband walked out on her." The messages we receive, along with the behavior we see modeled in those around us, mix in with our own trial-and-error attempts to grow up and make a life for ourselves. Those who study human behavior can detect the patterns that continue to be repeated as we live out a life script to its tragic or happy conclusions.

One who gets almost no healthy nurturing, who gets "you're bad" messages, who sees the acting out of abusive family relationships, will find that the easiest course in life is to believe the messages and act out the same kind of abuse. Breaking a script can be a painful (but liberating) experience. It involves learning what the script is, making a decision that life shall not be that way, and learning and practicing new patterns. Sometimes a person can complete this task with self-examination and willpower; often, especially in situations of persistent family abuse, one must have the intervention of a skilled therapist to discover and break the cycle.

Unhealthy Religion

Another contributor to abuse, we must admit, is un-healthy religion. The good news may be perverted into bad news by some who turn the teachings of the Old Testament and of Jesus into rigid rules. Some healthy and helpful guides for relationships may be exaggerated into distorted husband/ wife and parent/child relationships. The biblical guide for mutual submission may become exploitation; parental care may become parental smothering, leading to emotional crip-ples rather than strong, autonomous children. Church pro-grams and demands may lead to family neglect. We will look closer at the effects of unhealthy religion in family abuse in Chapter 3.

Fear for Survival

One of the most significant contributions to the abuse of other persons is the terrifying fear that one's own needs will not be met. The deepest needs of any of us are to be loved and cared for, to get attention and feel secure. The abuser may be the person who never received the quality or quan-tity of love and attention needed as a baby or young child, and therefore lacks self-esteem and confidence to grow to maturity. Or the abuser may have been overnurtured and not allowed to become independent and responsible. In either case, he or she is heavily dependent on other persons to meet basic needs for well-being and becomes desperately caught up in seeking need satisfaction. This seeking for affection and security feels like a life-or-death struggle for survival. He or she may turn to spouse or children to fill up the bottomless pit. No wonder persons in this desperate situation lash out at those expected to meet the impossible demands.

The Trigger—Stress

There is within each of us the potential for abuse, at some level, of those closest to us. Yet most persons go for long periods of time without any overt display of abusive behavior. What sets it off?

The usual trigger for abusive behavior is stress. I have found that the stress of a move can set off abusive behavior in my family. My wife and I are more likely to say and do things we regret later when we are physically tired from packing and carrying, emotionally drained from grieving over those we are leaving, preparing to make new friends, and tense from unexpected expenses and interrupted routines. Our needs for rest, for comfort, for reassurance are not being met, and we may lash out at the ones we most expect to help.

Stresses come in many forms. They may be physical illnesses, normal tiredness, financial strain, realistic or unrealistic worry, deaths, divorce, job loss. Stress may also come from very happy events. The birth of a child, a promotion on the job, graduation from school may all be very satisfying and fulfilling events, but they also call for changes in living patterns and adjustments to new challenges and opportunities. Any significant change requires energy and may be experienced as physical or emotional stress.

Researchers have discovered that the most stressful experiences for most people are closely related to family life— death of a spouse, divorce, separation, etc. Even relatively minor events, such as activities of the Christmas season or a vacation, are stress events. When a person's circuits are overloaded with too much stress, the consequences may be high blood pressure, heart disease, suicide—or family abuse. Often the trigger event preceding serious family abuse is a relatively insignificant act such as spilled food or a crying child. But this may be the last straw for a stress-overloaded person

How to Help

Each chapter in this book ends with a brief section entitled "How to Help." I have included suggestions for how to help yourself if you are caught up in abuse and how to help other persons you know with these problems. Here are some general principles covering the whole abuse scale.

How to Help Yourself

Look at Your Relationships with Others
Assuming you are as human as I, at times you do abuse some family members. Where is that misuse on the abuse scale? How serious is it? How far does it lean toward the neglect and violence end of the scale?

Look Within Yourself
How did family members use and misuse each other in the family in which you grew up? Where does that fit on the scale? What messages and scripts about your own life are you aware of?

Talk with Your Family
If your improper use of family members is rather low on the abuse scale, you may want to have a "family conference," or one-to-one conversations, to dialogue and decide how the quality of family life can be improved. If you tend toward the neglect and violence end of the scale, bring this problem out in the open and label it as a problem. Talk

about ways to change the patterns and thus relieve stress. Talk together about the possibility of seeking outside help.

Seek Professional Help

If family problems are unresolved after discussion and the trying of new behavior, seek the help of a counselor. Your pastor may be qualified to work with you or may refer you to a competent family counselor. Many communities have pastoral counseling centers or family counseling and mental health agencies that can be very helpful.

There will be problems to seeking professional help— perhaps embarrassment, fear of legal problems, lack of financial ability to pay for counseling. But remember—the well-being of *your* spouse, of *your* children, even *your own* well-being, is at stake. Don't let these obstacles keep you from getting the help you need for yourself and your family.

Seek God's Forgiveness

When we misuse God's creation, especially the crown of his creation, we have sinned against him. Convinced of sin, we need to repent and seek his forgiveness. We pray with the psalmist, "Create in me a clean heart, O God, and renew a right spirit within me," with the faith that he has power to make us new creatures. Not only does his forgiveness free us from the sting of sin; it gives us strength and courage for the difficult task of changing our behavior.

How to Help Others

Do Not Close Your Eyes to Reality
There are many sad situations of extreme abuse that have not been improved because no one wanted to get involved. You have "eyes to see and ears to hear." Use them!

Be Aware of Your State's Laws and Agencies
Many states have fairly recent laws relating to child and spouse abuse that encourage or even require the reporting of suspected incidents. Such laws are designed to push abusive persons to obtain help, rather than being designed for punishment. Many communities now have services and agencies that offer support and therapy to abusers and potential abusers.

Have a Network of Friends and Consultants
Abusive behavior is rarely black and white. The family member who abuses probably has a mixture of feelings, including love, guilt, and anger. You need some persons whose judgment you trust and with whom you can vent your feelings and get a clearer perspective on suspected abuse. You may be able to consult with some professionals to whom you might refer the abusive person for help.

Be Willing to Be a Friend
Abusive persons are often lonely, isolated individuals who try unsuccessfully to have all their needs met by spouse and children. Having outside friendships helps to ease this pressure. You may also be available to step in at times to baby-sit or otherwise give family members a break from each other and the stresses they face constantly.

Realize Your Own Humanity

Remember that "all have sinned and fall short of the glory of God," and that we must be aware of our own obstructions before removing the splinter in the eye of the other person. A self-righteous attitude toward abusers only pushes them to further isolation. A more helpful approach is to remember that we all stand under the judgment of God, redeemed only by his grace.

A Prayer for Forgiveness in Families

O Lord,
Forgive me, I pray, for my sins against my family;
   Forgive those times I have ignored them and neglected them;
      I was angry; I was preoccupied.
      Give me strength to ask their forgiveness.
Forgive those times I cut them with remarks, with chilling looks, with accusations;
   I was afraid; I was vengeful.
      Give me strength to ask their forgiveness.
Forgive those times I punished too hard, too long, too unjustly;
   I was consumed with anger; I was afraid of losing my power.
      Give me strength to ask their forgiveness.
Lord, I pray for grace to forgive their sins against me.
   Help me forgive them for not understanding;
   Help me forgive them for not seeming to care;
   Help me forgive them for not attending to me as I want and need.
      Give me courage to ask for what I want, and
      Give them strength to ask my forgiveness.
God of liberation,

Grant me freedom
   from the need to keep score,
   from the bondage of dependency,
   from the fear of responsibility,
And help me grow into full maturity in Christ,
  who loved us all
    and suffered the abuse of the cross
      that we might conquer sin and death
     and live a life of love in his name.
                   Amen

2. The Subtle Abuses

The lower end of the abuse scale is reserved for such problems as "ignoring," "withholding," "misusing." Though you are not likely to get arrested for such subtle abuses, they certainly keep you from living the "abundant life" that Jesus came to bring (John 10:10). The subtle abuses are quiet, little-noticed ways in which relationships deteriorate and self-images rot away. They may lead to more serious violations, or may simply result in loss of self-confidence and enthusiasm.

Why focus on abuses that are not serious enough to end up in court? There are several reasons.

1. The subtle abuses are like a low-grade fever: they are symptoms of a problem under the surface, but not dramatic enough to send you immediately for medical help. If unattended, however, they may lead to more traumatic abuse. How many steps are between the behavior of rudeness and the blow of spouse abuse? How far is it from emotional withdrawal to emotional neglect? Paying attention to subtle abuses is preventive of more obvious traumatic abuse.

2. The subtle abuses have all the characteristics of a mild chronic illness: loss of strength, loss of excitement and enthusiasm, low-grade depression and cynicism, and a gnawing away of the spirit. Why should you put up with a chronically

unhappy family life when you could be enjoying exciting, deeply satisfying family living?

3. The Scriptures teach that we are made in the image of God. To treat that image contemptuously is sin. How much abuse is necessary before we are guilty of sinning against the image of God in another person? Doesn't a little abuse tarnish the image as much as a lot? Surely God is displeased with even mild mistreatment of his creation.

KINDS OF SUBTLE ABUSE

Inconsiderateness

Perhaps the first abuse that creeps into most Christian families is inconsiderateness. My recent contact with a group of premarital couples has reminded me how preoccupied with each other and how utterly considerate a couple can be before marriage. It takes a good deal of time and energy to care tenderly for another person. Later, when children come, when job responsibilities increase, when unexpected stresses are faced, there simply is not the time and energy to be utterly devoted to each other. Each couple finds its own way to handle the shift away from attention to each other.

A common result is inconsiderateness. Husband and wife become less thoughtful. They drop their customary warm greeting and may neglect doing little unrequested favors. Often the offender is simply preoccupied with job or school or personal needs and may not be alert to the needs and desires of the spouse.

The writer of I Peter sensed the spiritual damage that can result from inconsiderateness. "Likewise you husbands, live considerately with your wives . . . since you are joint heirs of the grace of life, in order that your prayers may not be hindered" (I Peter 3:7). The inconsiderate spouse will find even prayer obstructed and unsatisfying!

Many a marriage that has lost its zip can be enlivened when one partner begins to pay more attention and contribute thoughtful acts and words. Our universal need for attention which says, "You're a special person to me," responds quickly to thoughtfulness. You can get a lot of mileage out of efforts to be considerate.

The Grudge

Another abuse that is a ready temptation is the holding of a grudge. Small irritations not quickly expressed may become festering sores. A cross word, an unkept promise, an unsatisfying sexual experience, an unthinking act may be planted in the soil of family relationships. Time and imagination help each blossom forth in hot anger or cold indifference.

Paul admonishes us not to let the sun go down on our anger (Eph. 4:26). This is good advice for a church fellowship, and even more indispensable advice for a family. When it comes to those inevitable irritations and slights in a family, "sufficient unto the day is the evil thereof" (Matt. 6:34). Today presents enough relationship problems without loading it down with the misunderstandings of yesterday.

The grudge is one of the behaviors basically contrary to Christian teaching. Grudging people do not forgive or forget. It takes time and energy to nurse a grudge—time not spent in loving or growing or serving. A relationship deteriorates in an atmosphere of begrudging.

Do an inventory of your grudges, active or dormant. How do they cause you to withhold yourself from your family? In what small ways do you find yourself "getting even" with a parent, a son, a daughter, a spouse?

Abuse by Idealism

An abuse particularly appealing to Christian families is the elevation of impossible ideals. You may feel so many "shoulds" and "oughts" that the freedom and excitement is starched out of your life. Further, you may live with such a load of unrealistic expectations, either of yourself or your family members, that guilt feelings overwhelm you. Some families seem to have an invisible judge whose approval can never be won. Parents communicate to children, and spouses to each other, "We are not living up to what we ought to be." This does not have to be an effort to "keep up with the Joneses" at all—it is more a constant failure to live up to the standards of the invisible judge.

Usually, when unrealistic ideals are glorified, certain areas of existence are not permitted or are severely restricted. Anger may not be permitted in any recognizable form; each family member is frustrated in attempts to deal openly with normal feelings about injustices and frustrations. Sexuality may be repressed. Your spouse may feel unable to be openly affectionate with you or with your children. Do your children receive degrading messages about their normal sexual interests and become stuck with feelings of fear and guilt? Ambivalence is not easily tolerated. The reality that you and I have both positive and negative feelings about every close person is not permitted. Family members are careful to show only the positive and put a lid on the negative.

The "bottom line" of abuse by idealism is a refusal to accept yourself and your family members as human. To be human is to be an uneven mixture of love and hate, of idealism and evil, of courage and cowardice. If you accept the limitations of being human, you can see your rightful place in God's creation—the crown of creation, yet a sinner in need of a Father's love and grace. Your task and mine is to be fully human. To want to be more is to try eating of the forbidden fruit; it is an old heresy dating back to the first century, that of denying our humanity in favor of a "purely spiritual" being.

Abuse of Privacy

A mother comes to the pastor upset because of what she has read in her fourteen-year-old daughter's diary. The daughter wrote of experiences she has not shared with her mother. She fantasized romantic adventures with an older boy. The mother presents this to the pastor with a question: Is my daughter sick, evil, or in need of a psychiatrist?

The pastor talks with the daughter and discovers that she has been daydreaming through her diary. Her interests are normal and healthy, but she is intensely furious with her mother for violating her privacy.

Each member of your family needs some space, a place, some area to call his or her own. To invade another's place without permission is to violate that person's rights and dignity. It indicates lack of trust: "I do not know what you may be hiding, so I'd better look (because you are probably up to no good)."

Smothering

Do you know the overwhelming feelings of affection and protection that come when you hold your own baby in your arms? The feeling is, "Whatever comes in life, I will protect you and prevent harm from coming to you." Later comes frustration when two-year-old has to do things "myself," even though "I could do it much quicker and less painfully."

You grow up with your children to some degree and realize that your job as a parent is not to protect them so they will never be touched by the roughness of life. You are to prepare them for whatever comes in life by letting them take on, as they are able, more and more responsibility and independence.

The smothered child is one whose every fall is cushioned, whose every encounter with people outside the family is orchestrated, whose very life is shielded from the normal rough-and-tumble of daily living. The smothered child is a hothouse plant who quickly wilts when put out in the realities of the outside world.

Some parents make it very difficult for their grown children to "cut the apron strings." You may find it hard to see your son or daughter take steps away from the family. There is a natural progression in which teenagers spend increasing amounts of time with dates and buddies and jobs and school. The goal of child-rearing is to give children the equipment to make it on their own as fully grown, competent adults. As the wedding approaches, or the trip off to college, or the first job, or the move into an apartment, you will have feelings of grief to deal with. In fact, things will never again be the same. But you also have much to celebrate! Let your gift to your sons or daughters at that crucial point be the gift of your blessing as they take their own places in the adult world.

The Ghetto

Families are abused by being forced to live in a ghetto. By definition, the ghetto is a place where people are confined, where it is difficult or even impossible to break out, where one mainly encounters people like oneself, and where the residents have very limited knowledge of the world outside the ghetto. Usually we think of the low-income ghetto, where it is very difficult to break out because of the cycle of low income, lack of education, lack of community leadership, poor housing and public facilities, etc.

You and I do not like the idea of living in a low-income ghetto because of the heavy feelings of oppression we have about it. "Ghetto" symbolizes the lowest level of economic survival, the necessity of living close to crime, and feelings of being imprisoned. Yet how quickly you and I who have decent incomes make ghettos out of suburbs. We create islands of middle-classness which, for the most part, isolate us from poor people, sick people, from urban and rural problems, from persons with different life-styles, and from some of the harsher aspects of life. Children raised in some suburbs find it hard to cope with the world, for the only world they know is fine homes, pampered lawns, and an overload of things. They also become "hothouse plants" who will wilt when exposed to an outside world which includes the poor, the rich, the physically ill, the mentally ill, the retarded, broken families . . .

Scapegoating

Once a year the ancient Israelites symbolically placed all the sins of the world on the head of a goat, then drove the goat out into the wilderness (Lev. 16:10). This was a way to free the people from the heavy burden of guilt by carrying the sin away from the guilty parties.

In the same way the burden of one's sin is often placed on some other family member. Young children, confronted with a broken lamp, will quickly insist, "Bobby did it." In more complex and devastating ways, a family begins to agree on which member gets the major blame for what goes wrong in the family. One person is labeled the "black sheep" or is identified as the "patient."

One old mountain custom is for friends and neighbors to bring food to the bedside of a newly deceased person. When all are gathered, the whole group turn their eyes as the "sin eater" comes to gobble the food and carry off as much as possible. This designated scapegoat lives as a hermit and is never to be seen by the rest of the community. The whole community values the function of the scapegoat, for the sins of the dead must be absorbed by someone.

What a destructive practice! Not only is the "sin eater" confined to no human contact or fulfillment, the rest of the community may feel relieved of taking responsibility for their own actions. The "black sheep" in the family is denied the advantage of being considered a person of worth and value, and other family members are relieved of responsibility for their own sins and shortcomings.

Who gets the blame in your family when you are unsure of the guilty party? Does some family member usually become suspect right away? Has your family decided that one member just doesn't measure up to the level of the rest of you?

The Curse

Verbal abuse may be quite mild and subtle, but nevertheless damaging. The Bible recognizes how powerful words are. The ancient Israelite threw his son to the ground so the curse of his enemy would go over the boy's head and not damage him. The word of blessing, uttered by Isaac to the wrong son, could not be withdrawn and given to Esau (Gen. 27:35).

The name of Jesus is to be highly exalted and to be the cause for every knee in the world to bow (Isa. 45:23; Rom. 14:11). When John wants to describe the action of God in Christ, he implies the power of the word—"the Word became flesh" (John 1:14).

One way of abusing with words is by *labeling* or *character assassination.* "You are no good." "You are clumsy." "You are not as smart as your sister."

Another is *persecuting by prophecy.* "You will never amount to anything." "You'll never be able to . . ." "If you keep on, you'll be pregnant before you're sixteen." These prophecies are self-fulfilling predictions. They help ensure that the future will be just as dire as predicted. A child or a spouse begins to feel, There is no use fighting, my fate is already sealed.

The persecuting prophecy borders on being a *curse.* Persons whose family members have placed a curse on them have a heavy burden to bear. "I wish you had never been born." "As far as I am concerned, I have no son. You are a stranger to me." "I never want to see your face again!" The curse may linger as a powerful skeleton in one's inner closet.

Abuse by Neglect

The Scriptures are clear about responsibility for the care of one's family. The Old Testament addresses relationships between husbands and wives, parents and children, and admonishes not only to care physically for family members but to teach the gracious acts of God. Jesus dealt with family relationships with tenderness and respect (as with Jairus' daughter, with Lazarus and his sisters). Paul summarizes the Christian attitude of care for one's family: "If any one does not provide for his relatives, and especially for his own family, he has disowned the faith and is worse than an unbeliever" (I Tim. 5:8). While devotion to God is primary in the Christian's life, one of the chief ways to express service in God's name is in families.

What are the needs of family members? What are the basics that family members deserve if they are not to be considered neglected?

One essential need is for *security.* Physical security involves food, shelter, health care. The man or woman who says to family members, "Be warmed and filled," but who does not provide the resources for being warmed and filled, is sinning against God and the family (James 2:15–16).

Another need of each family member is *emotional inti-*

macy. You and I are created with a need for closeness to others. Lack of that closeness has consequences ranging from physical disability to emotional starvation and identity confusion.

Fathers, especially, are tempted to be only "good providers" for the family and not to give of themselves. The workaholic father and the one who is always out with the boys is depriving his wife of needed affection and closeness and his children of a father's care and interest.

Obstetricians have recognized the importance of what they call "bonding" between parent and child. The initial contact between mother and child in the delivery room and the contacts later in the hospital room at feeding time are extremely important. If there is not close contact between parent and baby, and a calling forth of responses from each other, chances are increased for emotional problems and possible child abuse. "Bonding" is a good word to describe the needs that family members have for each other. We cannot live, or at least live well, without being bound to others who help us survive, discover identity, and launch out. It is interesting that the root meaning of the word "religion" is to bind or unite.

A less common form of neglect is *failing to discipline* in the sense of setting limits. Gerald's parents felt they were extremely progressive in their child-rearing practices. They gave their son no limitations, never corrected anything he did, and let him go where he wanted and when he wanted. The result? An obnoxious little boy who insisted on always having his way, who had no concept of the rights and feelings of others, who roamed the neighborhood without regard for personal safety. Deep down, Gerald felt alone and afraid; his behavior cried out for someone who would care enough to help him learn his limits.

Under the guise of waiting until Junior is older, or hoping

that he will never have to deal with certain issues, you may neglect to teach certain subjects. It is sticky to focus on conflictual relationships within a family, but the child who does not learn how to relate in the family will have a mammoth task trying to learn it outside. You may feel embarrassment when children ask questions about bodily functions, or specifically about sex; however, open teaching at this point can avoid much misinformation and unhealthy attitudes.

A final abuse by neglect is that of grown children who *refuse to honor their parents.* The sixth commandment, "Honor your father and mother . . ." was written to grown-up children, admonishing them to respect and care for aged parents. There comes a time when the roles are reversed as age brings diminished energy and income. The parents now need parenting from the child. You may be tempted to ignore aged parents or refuse to take responsibility for them. One common practice is for the siblings to designate one brother or sister, perhaps an unmarried one or the one who lives closest, to take care of the old parents. This puts an unfair burden on the "chosen one." There are no easy solutions for aging parents, but we are instructed to honor and care for those who earlier cared for us.

Misuse

It takes only a little reflection to realize that we use family members. There are legitimate and helpful ways you use other people—for instance, to meet your needs for love, security, and recognition. But the opportunity to use also means the opportunity to misuse. Misuse occurs when the other person is seen primarily as the means of meeting your needs without regard for the needs of that other person.

A common misuse in a family is constantly to *use a spouse as a parent.* It is healthy to take turns providing each other with nurturing, but sometimes one partner is forced to work overtime at it. A man may look to his wife to make major or minor decisions, provide security in the relationship, and set limits. She may get all the child-rearing responsibility and, in fact, respond to her husband as if he were a child. The same may happen with a wife who turns all decisions and responsibilities over to her husband. In this arrangement one spouse never grows up and the other always has to be grown up.

Another way to misuse family members is to *treat a child as a spouse.* Perhaps in a time of marital conflict, father turns to daughter, or mother to son, to meet intimacy needs. You begin to give your child attention, affection, and confidences that are more appropriate for a spouse. The results can be devastating. The marriage relationship suffers, and that causes confusion in children which may not be resolved for years. It is predestined to fail—a child simply cannot meet the needs of a parent.

A young man came for counseling because of constant arguments with his mother. His parents' marriage had drifted to a social and economic relationship with little affection or companionship. The husband was twenty years older than the wife, and they had little in common. She had turned her attention to this boy. Mother and son enjoyed gardening and music together and could talk at length about subjects of common interest, but the son found himself unable to break away at age twenty-eight. The only way he was able to differentiate himself from his mother was to declare a chosen life-style of homosexuality and to struggle to move finally into his own apartment.

Another temptation is to *fulfill your dreams through your children.* Junior league sports teams are filled with children who have no interest in the particular sport, but whose parents' needs are met through their son's or daughter's participation. Watch a peewee football team or baseball team play. Often there is more excitement in the stands than on the field. You may become so involved that the worth of your child—and of yourself—hangs on a touchdown play or a game-winning hit. The same dynamic operates in dance and music classes or in academic settings.

A particular temptation I have noticed in myself is the tendency to assume that my children will achieve no more than I did. Always an adequate but mediocre athlete, I realized recently I had been assuming that my son would be the same. I was putting a damper on my ten-year-old's dreams of a sports scholarship. While some parents may be tempted to fulfill dreams through their children, I was tempted to squash his dreams because of my experience.

Finally, a way to misuse family members is to *exercise parental power capriciously.* One father became known to his children mainly as a breaker of promises. Constantly he promised to take them to the movies or to the zoo, or have birthday parties, and then changed his mind or just did not show up. He laughed at their reactions and seemed to enjoy this expression of his power over them. His children now keep their distance, protecting themselves by not believing anything he says, and regard him with smoldering anger. Paul has a specific injunction against treating one's children this way: "Fathers, do not provoke your children to anger, but bring them up in the discipline and instruction of the Lord" (Eph. 6:4).

Subtle, but Sinful

The list could be longer. You and I are ingenious in finding ways to abuse family members. Subtle abuses will not usually result in jail sentences; sometimes you do not even consciously acknowledge that you are offending a family member. But through the years the subtle abuses grind on you and on your family relationships. They drain affection and joy, and end with chronic unhappiness. It is worth the effort to work on improving family relationships. Here are some guidelines.

How to Help Yourself

Realize that Subtle Abuse Is Universal

You and I will always have some problems in family relationships. We will always be tempted to abuse the rights and dignity of those closest to us when we feel threatened, anxious, or envious. Sometimes we will yield to temptation. A first step in dealing with family abuse is to realize you are not the only one by any means. As Paul discovered, each of us at times does not do the good we want to do, but the evil (Rom. 7:19). Some families may have fewer skeletons hiding in their closets than others have, and some may keep them better hidden, but no family is entirely free of subtle abuse.

Face Abuses

When you realize that your family is not the only one with problems—that, in fact, every family has similar struggles—you may be freer to admit yours and to deal with them. An ignored infection festers; as it is opened to the air and treated, it may be healed.

Grow from Coping

There is real strength and growth in a family that squarely faces its problems and finds ways to cope. Often the ideal presented of Christian family life implies that there is no conflict, no strain, no abuse. My concept of a healthy and well-functioning family is one in which each of the members learns to cope with the realities of differing expectations, conflicting needs, and rough edges in their relationships.

The children in such a home grow up with confidence that they can handle the problems that will inevitably come to them.

Confess and Seek Forgiveness

Sin is always ultimately against God. The psalmist emphatically stated, "Against thee, thee only, have I sinned" (Ps. 51:4). Jesus said whoever refuses to help "the least of these" has committed a sin of neglect against him (Matt. 25:40–46). Changing our abusive patterns starts with confession to God and prayer for his forgiveness.

Sinning against family members also needs repentance, confession, and request for forgiveness of the injured person. The Zacchaeus story tells us that the righting of relationship to God in Christ is followed by restoration of relationship to those we have injured (Luke 19:1–10). I disagree with a popular notion that "love means you never have to say you're sorry." Genuine love is grieved when the beloved is injured. We seek the forgiveness of those whom we love, that the relationship may be restored.

Examine Your Values

As you experience the forgiveness of God and seek to work out better relationships with family members, you will need to reexamine those values that put you in the abuser role. Do you subtly abuse family members because you hunger for power and authority? Do you feel threatened and have to reassure yourself that at least you are "boss" at home? Do you truly value the personhood and spirit of other family members? Is their welfare your deepest concern?

"The fruit of the Spirit is love, joy, peace, patience, kindness, goodness, faithfulness, gentleness, self-control" (Gal. 5:22–23). You and I can seek to stock our homes with an abundance of this fruit.

3. Religious Abuses in (and of) Families

Not only does abuse take place in Christian families; in some situations we must admit that Christians use religion to abuse, or at least use religion to justify abuses. Christian history is tarnished in places with accounts of Christian leaders, movements, and institutions that mistreated persons. The Crusades and the Inquisition stand out as prime examples. But even today abuses are taking place in the name of religion, and insensitive treatment of others is supported by reference to dogma and Scripture.

It is perversion of the worst sort to act contrary to the Spirit of Christ while claiming to do it for his sake. It is using the Lord's name in vain; it is hypocrisy of the first degree. To the extent that you and I are involved, we are part of the "whited sepulchres," empty tombs filled with deadness and uncleanness (Matt. 23:27). The greater tragedy is that, like the Pharisees, those who abuse by religion are often not even aware of the deadening results.

What are some of the ways religion may be used to abuse family members?

RELIGION AS A SWITCH

In some families in the area in which I grew up, the most fearsome threat that parents could use on their children was, "I'm going to get a switch!" A sturdy piece of hedge or a thin branch from a tree would be used across the seat and legs. It had only to be used once—after that, the threat of "getting a switch" was usually enough to produce obedience.

You may threaten with a religious "switch." "If you keep talking like that, Jesus is going to get you." Jesus is pictured as a boogeyman who is ready to leap on an offending child.

To a recently converted or confirmed family member, especially a child, you may say, "How can you call yourself a Christian if you . . ." In this way you reprimand the child for all kinds of behavior that may be natural and normal for the child's level of maturity. The message is, "Once you are a Christian, you have to stop being a child." Some children are told, "Honor your father and mother" in such a way that anything less than slavish obedience is considered sin against parents and God.

Religion may be used to club adult family members as well. One woman, convinced that her husband was dissolute and hopeless, used every opportunity to quote Scripture and sermons to remind him of his worthlessness. She occasionally asked her pastor to speak to the husband. The request was to help the husband, but the underlying feeling tone was, "Sic him!"

The message of the switch is not love or reason or education. It communicates, "I am bigger, I can hurt you, so you had better obey." This religion of fear contrasts with a God who "so loved the world that he gave his only Son" (John 3:16).

A switch is feared and hated. As soon as a person under

the threat of the switch feels strong enough, that abused person will attempt to throw the switch away or break it in rebellion.

CHURCH ABUSE OF FAMILIES

Churches are institutions with all the potentialities for good and evil of other institutions. One important requirement of any institution or organization is that it be able to sustain itself. It needs a certain amount of leadership, financial resources, participation, and territory. When a church gets beyond the survival level in these areas, it may turn its attention to more "noble" ventures, such as missions and ministries outside itself in enabling its congregation to grow into mature Christian disciples.

The family, too, needs a minimum level of leadership, energy, finances, and territory. Churches contribute to family abuse when institutional needs are put ahead of needs of families and individuals. Church leaders may equate goals of the church with goals of the Kingdom of God and demand for the church a loyalty that is to be reserved only for God himself. At this point the church may contribute to family abuses in several ways.

Time and Energy Abuse

The most frequent sort of family abuse perpetrated by churches involves the expenditure of time and energy. Churches have a way of scheduling the calendar full of church activities. I have been on church staffs and participated in church planning meetings where we became concerned if there was any major or minor event which occurred without some church activity related to it. We wanted to give our members—especially our young people —something "Christian" to do at all times. We acted as if

activities sponsored by schools, scouts, clubs, and neighbor-
hoods would be detrimental to our people. We had to give
them a Christian setting for everything. Thus we had after-
game parties, New Year's Eve activities, after-prom activities, banquets, vacation trips, retreats, etc. All this, of course,
was in addition to regularly scheduled programs several days
and nights a week, and all day every Sunday.

Besides the commitment asked from regular members,
such a schedule requires an enormous amount of time and
energy from leaders. Since competent leaders are at a pre-
mium in most churches, the same persons will be leading
several major projects at once.

Have you seen this subtle abuse happen in your church?
Husbands/fathers are tied up most of Sunday, have commit-
tee meetings two or three nights a week, may be asked to
be part of a Saturday project, and feel pressure to do even
more. Wives/mothers may be involved in these meetings
and, if not working outside the home, be in women's group
meetings and expected to lead and chauffeur after-school
activities. In a few extreme cases I have seen, it would be
appropriate to call the children of such parents "church
orphans."

Children, as well, may be involved in regular church
meetings and several children's or youth activities a week.
Members of the family may become strangers to one another and find themselves avoiding intimate dialogue for
long periods of time.

Insensitivity to Family Needs

One of the ways in which churches contribute to family
abuse may be seen as a sin of omission. There are churches
of all brands where the needs of individuals and families are
not addressed. The church may be focused on evangelism,
or on social justice, or on any of a score of other good causes,

and miss the opportunity to minister right under its nose.

Many churches, for instance, are still acting as if all families consisted of a mother, a father, and two children. However, in the United States today, one third of all children do not have both natural parents in the home. The number of one-parent families is rapidly increasing, as are the number of single adults and childless couples. These persons need special attention to their family relationships. Even in the healthiest of two-parent families there are needs that the church can address as husband/father, wife/mother, and children grow and change. The needs are intensified by divorce, death, crime, or violence.

The church that fails to establish some sort of care and learning experience for its members in relation to their family life is failing to address the gospel at the place where it is hardest to live the gospel. We are letting the sheep wander around in the wilderness without a shepherd.

Some churches are developing programs of family living that deal with each age level according to need. Guidance in Christian attitudes toward the family, dealing with conflict, Christian views of sexuality, and intimacy growth are possible. Families can be introduced to community resources that are available for counseling and material help. An attitude of love and sensitivity can be extended to the single person, the divorced person, the one-parent family. Grief education and counseling can support persons through difficult family losses.

Abuse by Sanctification

An especially tempting abuse in churches may be called "abuse by sanctification." In a well-meaning attempt to present the gospel with all of its demands and promises, church leaders sometimes go overboard with their expectations for daily living. An ancient heresy (gnosticism), which arbitrarily separates the physical from the spiritual, creeps in. Some in the church, it is assumed, have not sinned, except in the dim, distant past. Ideals held up before Christians are unrelated to the struggle of earthy, day-to-day living.

A reflection of this abuse is the division into camps in a church. One group begin to assume that they are God's favorite ones because life is going well for them. Another group may become competitively proud and claim favoritism themselves. A third group, realizing the futility of reaching the inflated standards, despair of the gospel having any help or hope for them.

Paul is one who held up the high standards of Christian conduct, yet who knew the futility of striving for unrealistic perfection. Romans 7 is a picture of a man who struggled with his desire to do the right thing, but who continually failed to keep the law. Only through the strength of the Lord Jesus could he find help (Rom. 7:25). The home is the place where it is most difficult to take seriously and live out fully the demands of the gospel. What happens to *agape* when a parent is up all night for the third night in a row with a cranky child? How many times can we forgive a family member who seems grossly insensitive to our needs?

Churches abuse families when they hold up an unrealistically high ideal that is unrelated to the nitty-gritty of everyday family life. According to the pictures drawn in some pulpits and some Sunday school classes, every mother is a madonna, every child is a cute and cuddly bundle of joy, and every father is a tender and compassionate tower of strength.

Another way in which extravagant expectations of the church are an abuse is in making persons feel guilt over lack of faith. A young man lay dying of a brain tumor. His parents and wife had gathered for a vigil at the hospital. The family's grief and guilt were intensified when a few distant family members and a minister urged them to pray for healing—and implied strongly that if the patient died, it would be because of their lack of faith.

High standards of Christian life and faith must be tempered with compassion and common sense.

Parent-Child Dependency

In folk religion much emphasis is placed on self-sacrificing mothers and submissive children. Mothers are expected to give their all for their children and in return to receive honor and even adoration. Children are to be humble and obedient and compliant. Fathers are more distant and vague, although there is also a picture of them as being all-knowing, strong, and distantly compassionate.

Folk religion would have us believe that the birth of a child begins an unbroken period of joy and happiness and good family times until the death of the aged parents in the home of their children. There is no recognition of the need for children and parents to be independent of each other. The pilgrimage from babyhood to adulthood is marked by several stages of increasing autonomy. Infants need parents to feed, change, clothe, and shelter them. But as the two-year mark approaches, children begin to assert their own personalities and independence of spirit.

The only mention in the Scriptures of the life of Jesus between birth and manhood is the story of the trip to Jerusalem. The twelve-year-old Jesus declared his independence from his parents—"I must be in my Father's house" (Luke 2:49). It is interesting that later Jesus encourages a man to leave his parents and follow him (Luke 9:59–60) and that he recognizes the need for a person to leave parents in order to be married. Jesus himself considered those who heard and kept God's word to be closer to him and more blessed than his own family (Luke 8:19–21; 11:27–28).

Social Pressure

A young pastor in a small rural church became concerned about a family that regularly attended services. The mother and three young children were always there on Sunday mornings. It was obvious that the mother was not very bright and that the children were impulsive. The pastor and some other church leaders became concerned, for whenever the children squirmed or talked above a whisper during the service, the mother would give them a loud whack and sometimes a verbal threat. It was disturbing to persons around her, and the strength of her physical punishment caused concern about the children. If she was this severe with them in public, what happened when she had them alone at home?

While wondering whether to report this to the county authorities, the pastor and his wife were invited to this woman's home for Sunday dinner. Much to their surprise they had a very pleasant and enjoyable afternoon. At home this mother was warm, caring, and openly affectionate with her children. An obvious bond of mutual love highlighted the relationship of mother and children.

The pastor surmised that this woman basically loved and cared tenderly for her children. She felt a heavy burden of expectation while at the church. Her interpretation of subtle messages from the church was that children should never make noise or movement that would disturb the worship service. Her anxious desire that her children be well thought of came out in excessive sensitivity to their natural squirming and whispering.

The pastor was able to interpret her behavior to church members who were upset by it, and to reassure this anxious mother that her children were accepted and wanted in church even when they squirmed.

Another kind of social pressure is economic. We often communicate where we are economically by how we dress. Those who are not able to dress as nicely as others may feel uncomfortable and unwanted in a particular church. Some will search until they find a church where they can be comfortable; some will just drop out altogether.

EXAGGERATED INTERPRETATIONS

The way we use other persons in the family may be the result of overdoing a good thing. For instance, some people have advised women to be utterly subservient to their husbands. Paul begins his section in Ephesians on family relationships by saying, "Be subject to one another out of reverence for Christ" (Eph. 5:21). Paul admonishes wives to be subject to their husbands, then directs twice as much instruction to husbands to nourish and cherish their wives (Eph. 5:23–31). One spouse may use either emphasis in this passage from Scripture to justify tyrannical behavior. In the same way, parents are admonished to train their children in the way they should go and to discipline them in the Lord. This advice also becomes a weapon in the hands of a parent who, deluded into thinking of himself or herself as a god, demands rigid conformity to commands. "Honor your father and mother" comes as a rigid command, with "honor" being interpreted as strict obedience.

In like fashion the admonition to care for families may be exaggerated into justification for an unhealthy overdependency. Mother provides for baby's every need, and continues to insist on responding to every need of the child as it becomes older. Mothering becomes smothering, and the child is never given the chance to become autonomous and self-reliant.

One father distorted the biblical admonition to witness and lead others to salvation by focusing on his five-year-old son. The boy was commanded to confess his sins every night and not to fall asleep until he did. He is now grown, and a vivid memory from his childhood is of lying awake many hours each night trying to think of sins to confess. Partly because of this kind of fearful teaching, he is now a constricted and compulsive young man, lacking spontaneity and creativity.

LEGALISM

Another reason for abuse is unhealthy religion. The God and Father of our Lord Jesus Christ is a God of health, of growth, of life, freedom, and responsibility. He calls us to grow toward full maturity as Christian persons, to be fully the human beings he has intended, made in his image.

But many have perverted faith from a relationship with a living God to a set of rules and regulations that are rigidly enforced. Differences in ages, stages of development, and unique personality traits are ignored. Above all, the rules must not be broken; if they are broken, punishment must be swift and sure (and sometimes is permanently destructive).

In one Christian home, a fourteen-year-old son was found breaking a minor rule of the household. For the next two weeks, rather than being allowed to go out with his friends, he had to stay in the house after school and read twenty chapters of the Bible every day. The smoldering anger of this son would be stored up and would burst into flames at some later provocation.

How to Help Yourself

Pray

Our lives as Christians are grounded in relationship to God. Keep that relationship alive through frequent prayer and a prayerful attitude. Try listening for God's movement in your life, watch for his direction, be open to his confrontation. In a time of meditation on your life, on the messages of Scripture, and on the love of God for you and your family you may see more clearly your tendencies to misuse your faith.

Study the Scriptures

Get in touch with more and more of the Scriptures that are unfamiliar to you. Immerse yourself in the Gospels, study Paul's interpretations and admonitions, and read the prophetic visions of love and peace and righteousness of the Old Testament. Let the Bible be a guide and confronter in your use of religious doctrine and personal faith.

Seek Christian Fellowship and Guidance

Often the abuse of families by religion is tied to a lack of spiritual support and maturity. You are a grown man or woman, yet you may be a small child in the faith. Look to the church for fellowship and growth. Look especially to those who have admirable qualities of Christian maturity. When you find a person who seems sincerely committed, has a strong relationship with God, and has a depth of understanding of self and others, give weight to that person as a model and guide for you.

Confess and Seek Forgiveness

Taking God's name in vain does not refer primarily to cursing. We abuse God's name by treating the things of

God profanely or hypocritically. You and I need to confess those times when our faith becomes a switch or a club or mainly a shield. Confession to God in prayer and to the injured party can open the door for forgiveness and restoration.

How to Help Others

Refrain from Burdening Others

Jesus' anger was directed toward those who had burdened others with cumbersome religious duties and did not lift a finger to help them carry the burden (Matt. 23:4). The good news is that Jesus has saved us from our sins, given us freedom and love, and opened the doors to maturity and abundant life. Let us refrain from spreading the bad news of guilt and oppression by religion.

Confront Others

There come times when it is needful to help our brother or sister by speaking the truth in love. When one burdens another unnecessarily, or when one seems to create more and more burdens until the other person's back and spirit are broken, the word of truth in love is needed.

It is easy to load burdens on others, for it often seems that we desperately need to keep the institution going, or our own ego afloat. It is likewise easier to carry heavy burdens than to face the freedom of choice and action that Jesus gives us. Yet we need to be loving confronters of each other; burdens of loving and caring are heavy enough without our wasting energy on unnecessary loads.

Serve as a Model

You may be a model for others as you reach a level of maturity and leadership. As you demonstrate both true devotion and true freedom, you may help other persons learn to live their lives with greater dependence on the grace of God. You may help others understand by your example what it means to love one's neighbor as oneself.

PART

II

FOR SEVERE ABUSERS
(and Those Who Would Help Them)

4. Child Abuse

Child abuse? In a book directed to the Christian family?

Yes, child abuse is a widespread problem of tragic proportions which reaches into many homes—even Christian homes. Christian parents are subject to the frustrations, unhappy childhood, and isolation that lead to abusing children.

In spite of the widespread publicity given child abuse since the early 1960's, many people are still unaware of what actually happens to children, why it happens, and what can be done about it. Some of this general information is presented in this chapter addressed to the abusing parent.

THE PROBLEM

As with other kinds of social problems being highlighted today, it is difficult to say whether child abuse is increasing or whether it is only public knowledge that is increasing. From a Christian perspective, it would be tragic if only one child were abused. Actual figures reveal that hundreds of thousands of cases of abused children are reported every year and it is estimated that at least as many more cases are unreported. Child abuse deaths are in the thousands annually.

Child abuse is not a new occurrence. In most ancient civilizations the killing of infants was regarded as a legitimate means of birth control or of increasing the ratio of male children to female children. Children were considered the property of their parents, who had few restraints on the manner in which they treated their children. In the 1960's, sociologists and psychologists began to study the problem extensively. The result has been new terms such as "battered child syndrome" and the development of organizations and agencies to help abused children and abusing parents.

Child abuse is any nonaccidental injury to a child's body or to the child's emotional, intellectual, or spiritual development. *Child neglect* is the failure to provide what a child needs for physical, emotional, intellectual, or spiritual growth and normal development. Some illustrations will help you identify the behavior (or lack of behavior) included.

Physical abuse involves injuring a child by severe whipping, beating, or throwing. The child subjected to physical abuse may have bodily marks and bruises from belts, rulers, sticks, or hands. The child may have fractures, burns, cuts, or sores. This kind of abuse may go on for years or may end in the child's death. Physical neglect includes malnutrition resulting from lack of adequate food, unattended illnesses, inadequate clothing, and untreated dental problems.

Emotional abuse may accompany physical abuse, but it also occurs without any physical injury. The parent may "smother" the child by too much attention and stifling of freedom. The parent may engage in constant "character assassination": "You'll never amount to anything." "You're evil." Emotional neglect is lack of recognition of a child's existence, needs, and wants. This may lead to intellectual neglect, that is, the parent expects far too much or far too little of the child intellectually. In conditions of emotional abuse and neglect, the child gets the message that he or she is bad, unwanted, and unimportant.

Sexual abuse is an especially insidious problem which involves both physical and emotional abuse. A child is not ready for sexual relations either physically or emotionally. Sexual abuse includes sexual relations of a child with a parent, stepparent, foster parent, or sibling. It may involve intercourse, exposure, fondling, or sodomy. Sexually abused children may have physical injuries. They may also have many emotional obstacles to healthy growth and development. They wonder: "Am I evil? Will anybody ever love me just for me? Can I have a normal marriage when I grow up?" They may be burdened with an awful secret they cannot share.

Children respond in a variety of ways to abuse and neglect. Some become very passive and withdrawn, even mute. Some become very aggressive and combative. Some act out in delinquent behavior. Some develop mental disorders. Most never learn to play. And some die.

Factors in Child Abuse

Child abuse does occur in this less-than-perfect world, even in Christian families. I am now writing directly to you who find yourself caught up in the cycle of abuse. It may help you to know some of the common experiences in the circumstances and histories of abusing parents. All these factors may have a part in your experience. Most likely some of them have particular importance in influencing the way you act.

Background of Abusing Parent

Look into your own childhood through your memory and through conversations with older family members. Were you abused or neglected?

A high percentage of abusing parents were themselves abused as children. It is true of parents that they tend to treat their children the way they were treated. That is only natural, since this is the way they learned how to relate to children. Unless you have deliberately looked for other parenting models, the way you were disciplined as a child may be the only way you know to deal with your own child.

The feelings you have about the way you were treated also play a part in your parenting attitudes and behavior. If you were unfairly or severely punished or constantly ignored, you may have tremendous anger under the surface. That anger is loosed when your own child displeases you. If you do not think through your behavior about raising your child, you may be living by a twisting of the Golden Rule: "Do unto others as you were done unto."

A student minister with whom I worked had been abused as a child by a father who was unmerciful with his belt. As this young man grew up, he realized the unfairness of the way he had been treated. He began to fear that he could not marry and have children because he might repeat the cycle of abuse. Finally he sought counseling and began a study of different ways of parenting. He awaits the birth of his first child with some anxiety, yet with confidence that he has prepared for parenthood, and that he knows of resources in case he needs more help. He is aware of God's help in his struggle to become a father whose actions reflect the love of the heavenly Father.

That is the answer for you who were abused as a child and sincerely want to avoid repeating the abuse. Seek help to deal with your history and to learn new ways of parenting. It will cost you time and energy, but the outcome could be eternally satisfying for you and your children.

Insecurity and Low Self-Esteem

Most abusing parents have little self-esteem and a large need for approval. You may feel deep down that you are worth little, that you are unlovely and unlovable. This kind of anxiety sometimes leads to a desperate desire to be perfect. You feel that you cannot make any mistakes, or that you will not be approved of by those who are important to you. This extends to your children. You feel greatly threatened when your child is slow to be toilet trained, wets the bed, is not polite to adults, does not learn quickly—in short, does not measure up to whatever you expect. It becomes a test of your parenting. You feel you will not be approved of if your children do not measure up.

In your great need for approval, you may turn to your child. You may expect your child to give you the love and appreciation and security that you feel unable to get from adults. Your child may have to act very grown up and learn to reassure you constantly and take care of you. You may be trying to create a parent for yourself from your child. This has sad consequences for both of you. You miss out on the adult companionship you need. Your child misses out on the opportunity to be a child, to learn to play, and to assume responsibility gradually. You are giving your child a task that a child could not possibly accomplish.

Unrealistic Expectations

A great number of parents abuse their children mildly or severely because they expect behavior from a child that the child cannot produce. "He's just being stubborn." "She's deliberately doing that (to ruin my day)." It makes you furious when a child seems to be failing you.

These unrealistic expectations may start on the day the baby comes home from the hospital. You expect a warm, cuddly "bundle from heaven" that will constantly coo and smile and be the joy of your life. You find, instead, that the "bundle from heaven" times are rather rare. Much of the early months of parenthood are consumed with wet and smelly diapers, interrupted sleep, and loss of freedom. Baby's crying can be especially hard to handle. Babies usually cry for good reasons—to signal the need to be fed, changed, or held—but sometimes the reason is impossible to find. Frustration and anger can build, and if it is not drained off in some constructive way, you may begin abusing the baby by hitting or neglecting in an effort to stop the crying.

Toilet training is another issue that sometimes leads to abuse. Many parents do not have the information that little girls' bodies are ready for bowel and bladder control at about age two and little boys' at about age three. With a minimum of time and teaching, most children quickly learn control at these ages. Earlier attempts are often a huge waste of time and energy, and leave both parent and child greatly frustrated and feeling inadequate. I have talked with parents who were disturbed that their baby at nine months was not yet toilet trained, and even with one young mother who felt she had to start at three months! These unrealistic expectations, in combination with some of the other factors mentioned in this section, may lead to child abuse. You may have your feelings of inadequacy and anger greatly expanded by a struggle to get a child to conform to behavior of which he or she is simply not capable.

Unrealistic expectations extend beyond the preschool years. Parents who are uninformed about normal growth and development will have problems all along the way by not knowing what to expect or how much freedom to allow. This is especially difficult with the first child; the parent has had no previous experience. My wife and I were overly concerned about each phase of growth of our first son. We relaxed much more with our second and third children, for we knew more of the normal course of development and could gauge better when to be worried and when to be relaxed. A friend who has raised four children says that no one should have a first child; we should all start with the second!

Even though you do not have the option of starting with the second child, there are ways to adjust your expectations to reality. One is to communicate with other parents and find out how they are managing parenting problems. Another is to seek specific information from a professional, such as a doctor, minister, nurse, or social worker. Another is to read one or more of the helpful books that discuss the normal growth and development of children at each age.

Unrealistic expectations are not confined to children. You may have expectations of your spouse that are way out of line. You may expect more in the areas of money, child care, or emotional support than is realistic. Feeling let down by your spouse, you may turn your anger on your children.

You may expect far too much from yourself. The traditional picture of the always giving, never complaining, constantly smiling parent may be a real burden for you. Nobody ever told you about the huge amount of giving that is required in parenthood, about the need to get away at times, about the desirability of having some identity of your own apart from your children. You may have some very natural and normal feelings of anger, resentment, and being trapped that you feel are unacceptable.

Isolation

A common feature in the lives of most abusing parents is social isolation and loneliness. Several problems are aggravated when you do not have meaningful relationships with other persons. You do not get your needs met for affection and companionship. It is hard for you to feel affirming and caring and loving when you are not being affirmed and cared for and loved by other people.

Another problem of isolation is that it deepens any sick aspects of relationships within your family. If abuse or neglect of some kind is happening, you need to realize that there are many other families in which this does not take place. Seeing other families relate will give you some better perspective on how your family could change.

Isolation also keeps you from checking your expectations against those of other parents. When do they begin toilet training their children? How far do they let the eight-year-old go from home? In what ways do they discipline their children? What do they expect of themselves? How do they handle their own feelings of inadequacy and frustration?

A good way to break out of isolation and the problems it causes is to become part of a group of abusing parents, such as Parents Anonymous. Here you can make friendships, realize that you are not the only person involved in this problem, and discuss better ways to parent your children.

Defective Parenting Attitudes

Some abuse and neglect is the result of ideas and attitudes about parenting that disregard Scripture, psychological insights, and common sense. These ideas, put into practice by well-meaning persons, often result in just the opposite of what is desired.

One of these defective attitudes is that *children are property.* The interest of other people in your children may anger you: "They're my children, I'll do with them what I want."

The attitude that children are parental property has been widespread since ancient times. This way of thinking has led to emotional crippling, physical abuse, and even murder. In contrast, the Scriptures teach that children are not property, but a gift from God. A child is a blessing (Ps. 127:3–5).

Parents have the responsibility to protect, nurture, teach, and strengthen children (Deut. 11:19)

Christians are to be good stewards of the gifts that God entrusts to them. God gives us small, unformed, fragile babies. We can give back fully grown men and women who are fulfilling their potential for being responsible, independent, compassionate adults.

Another defective parenting attitude is that *parental authority is sacred.* It is important to have leadership in the family, and there are times when parents must stand firm, even though the discipline and decisions are unpopular. Yet you may be so impressed with the command, "Honor your father and mother" that you make obedience to your will a sacred duty. This tends to put you in the place of God. To God alone is ultimate obedience and commitment due. Notice the lives of Joseph, David, and Jesus in their younger years. There was not strict obedience to an authoritarian parent, but a dialogue of conversation and action. Jesus in the Temple at age twelve was already exercising some freedom from his parents and giving loyalty to a higher authority (Luke 2:41–51). Your children need increasing opportunities to assert their independence, and even rebelliousness, as they discover who they are under God.

If you feel that parental authority is sacred, then the child who talks back to you and is disobedient is not just acting against you, but against God. You then feel obligated to use any means to force this child into conformity. A defective parenting attitude which often accompanies this one is that *my child will turn out "evil"* if I do not force the child to conform.

A middle-aged couple with five children gave up a secure job and home because the husband felt called to the ministry. They lived in a trailer while the father went to a Bible college nearby. One teenage daughter began to declare her independence by complaining about having to attend frequent, long church services. The parents came to feel she was the one bad child in the family and must be forced into conformity at any cost. Daily beatings with hands and a belt were climaxed by a severe whipping when she was caught smoking while the rest of the family were in church. Brought to court over the matter, the parents insisted on their God-given right to treat their children as they wanted, especially this "evil" child.

Another defective parental attitude is summarized by the biblical admonition, *"Spare the rod and spoil the child."* Like some other passages of Scripture, this one has been misinterpreted and exalted to the level of divinity itself by some persons. It conveys to you the idea that if you do not physically punish your child, you are somehow failing your responsibilities as a parent.

The truth in this verse is that a parent is failing the child when the parent refuses to give firm guidance and discipline. You probably know a child whose parents have refused to parent. The child is without limits; out of a great sense of insecurity, he or she becomes "spoiled rotten," constantly whining or acting obnoxiously or in some other way begging for limits.

The other side of the coin is parents who feel that a child needs "a good licking" at least once a week. You may be caught in a double bind: guilt feelings when you whip your child, for you sense you are overdoing it; and guilt feelings when you do not, for you feel you are not being a good parent. Whipping usually does more harm than good. There are better ways of teaching your child.

A closely related parental attitude that is defective is that *discipline and punishment are identical.* Discipline comes from the word for teaching. We discipline children to teach them—to teach them their limits, to teach them respect for other persons and property, to teach them confidence and self-reliance and cooperation. Punishment, on the other hand, has more the meaning of inflicting a penalty, handling roughly, or hurting. It is not necessarily fair and does not always produce the desired results. Punishment may be inflicted to teach a child an important lesson, but the goal is the learning of the lesson, not the experience of the punishment.

For instance, if you want to teach your children respect for others and care for them, how do you do it? When Johnny hits Billy, you can whip Johnny and lecture him about not hitting people. But you have taught Johnny through your actions that the way to handle people who cross you is to hit them. The way of discipline would depend on Johnny's age and maturity. For three-year-olds who are fighting over the only ball in the house, it might be to show them a simple game they could play together with the ball. For a ten-year-old who had broken a neighbor's window, it might be confessing to the neighbor and earning money to replace the window.

● What do your children learn from the way you treat them when you are unhappy with their behavior? Do they learn the lessons you intend to teach—respect for authority, good manners, cooperative behavior—or do they learn that parents must be obeyed because they are bigger and can hit harder? Picture your child in twenty years. Do you want your grandchildren to be treated the way you treat your child?

STRESS—THE TRIGGER

Whatever the history of a particular parent and the current life circumstances, there is usually a stressful situation that triggers an actual incident of abuse. You may be able to maintain an even keel during smooth times in your life, but when the rough waves come, you begin lashing out at those close to you.

When you are under intense stress, especially if it persists for a long period of time, your coping resources begin to fail you. You may be physically exhausted, emotionally drained, unable to see the "light at the end of the tunnel." In those times the normal irritations of family life seem very large and threatening. You may even feel that your whole world is collapsing. You punish your child too hard, too long, or you ignore your child's physical or emotional needs.

The following are some common stresses that trigger child abuse.

Financial Crises

Financial trouble is no respecter of persons. Parents at or near the poverty level have obvious struggles to find and maintain adequate food, shelter, and clothing. Those in middle-income groups are having their real income eaten away by higher taxes, inflation, and enticements to buy (or charge) more and more. Those at the highest income levels make decisions and investments that could reverse their fortunes in a short time.

One husband and wife worked hard and finally achieved "success": a home in a high-class neighborhood, two new cars, and high salaries for both of them. Yet within a few months of moving into their new home they discovered that the mortgage payments required half their income and car payments were taking most of the rest. They felt great pressure to buy their children clothes like the neighbor children had, go on vacations like the family next door, and tithe to their church. Unable to meet their obligations, and falling further into debt every month, they truly felt poor in spite of their surroundings. Marital quarreling from financial stress spilled over into child abuse.

Lack of adequate money in comparison with needs (and wants) can mean much more than lack of food on the table. Your sense of personal adequacy, independence, power, and self-worth may be closely involved with lack of money.

Problem Children

Studies have revealed that children who are unusual problems to their parents are candidates for child abuse. If you have a problem child, your temptation to abuse is greater.

The premature baby who spends several weeks or months in the hospital after birth may be a real drain on the family. Medical costs can be overwhelming. Trips to the hospital take much time and energy. The child may remain small and sickly for several years. Parents miss out on the "parental bonding" stage, that important development of belonging and attachment between parent and infant in the first few hours of life.

If your child is mentally retarded, there is a greater chance of abuse. You have to give up some of your dreams for this child when the reality of retardation hits you. You may still be experiencing some grief about your child being slower or less intelligent than others. A retarded child may be dependent on you for a longer period of time; this results in frustration for you and anxiety about the child's care when you are gone.

Physically ill or handicapped children also are problem children for a parent. You may find that vast amounts of your time, energy, and money are invested in the child. You might be neglecting your own needs and those of your spouse and other children to care for the sick child.

Physical or emotional neglect is a temptation when you are faced with a problem child. Just the opposite is also a possibility—smothering the child with excessive attention and protection. It is a curious pattern of us human beings that we sometimes become afraid of our feelings and act just the opposite of our deepest feelings. We may be oversolicitous of our child, attend to his or her every need and want, and not give the child the opportunity to grow up and be independent. Smothering leads to an emotionally dependent, and sometimes crippled, adult.

Illness

I have already mentioned how the illness of a child creates stress. Parental illness is also a stressful condition. Your own illness is difficult, draining physical and emotional energy, making it harder to cope. When your spouse is sick, it compounds any preexisting problems of finances and lack of mutual help. You not only have your regular responsibilities within and outside the family, you also have the drain of nursing a sick mate at home or making many trips to the hospital. Anxiety over your spouse's condition adds to the problem. It is difficult to express frustrations and resentment to a sick person. Your frayed nerves and frustration naturally make you more irritable, and perhaps abusive, with your children.

Trapped Feeling

While either parent may feel trapped by the circumstances of life, usually a mother has fewer opportunities to get away from the burdens of parenthood. While you enjoy your children at times, it is very difficult to get away from the constant responsibility. Even when you get away for an evening out or for a short trip, there is a huge amount of preparation so that whoever is keeping the children will know the routines and quirks of each child.

You may be oppressed with the notion that a mother should never leave her children, even for short periods.

With no relief, small demands feel like large demands, and routine work becomes drudgery. It begins to seem as if it is your child's fault that you are trapped at home with no escape. Your child may begin to bear the brunt of your feelings of being abused and neglected as you abuse and neglect your child.

The solution is regular periods of relief from responsibility. Your spouse may take over and give you some free time. You might hire a baby-sitter. You might trade off child care with a friend. You might leave your child for short times in one of the many fine "Mother's Day Out" programs in churches.

When you feel trapped and abused or neglected, it will seep out in your parenting.

Nonsupportive or Absent Spouse

You have an extra burden if your spouse is not supportive of you personally, does not share the burden of parenting with you, or is absent because of separation or death. Parenting is a difficult job in the best of circumstances with two parents. If your spouse is not participating because of a lack of concern or because of absence, your stress is multiplied.

Young Parents

Parenting is a task for adults, but thousands of teenagers become parents every year. If you are very young and already have a child, you face the problem of a lack of knowledge and a lack of maturity that would help you to face the task. In addition, you may not have finished your own developmental tasks of childhood and adolescence. You feel frustrated and resentful when your friends go out and enjoy themselves and you are stuck at home changing diapers.

If you are older but were married at a young age, you may

feel that your youth was cut short. These kinds of feelings sometimes lead to marital quarreling, divorce, or child abuse.

Alcohol and Drug Addiction

Alcohol aggravates any tendencies toward abuse. It clouds your good judgment, takes away needed inhibitions, and magnifies your problems. A large majority of abusive incidents happen while a parent is under the influence of alcohol. You may not even realize you have abused your child until much later when the alcoholic cloud lifts.

Your addiction to alcohol or drugs may be so strong that you are totally consumed with getting these substances. You have no money or time or attention left for your child. My hope is that something will shock you into the realization of your destructive behavior and your need for help.

How to Help Yourself

Child abuse is serious. It damages your child physically and emotionally. It damages your feelings about yourself and your relationships to others. At some point, without intending it, you could go too far and your child could be permanently disabled or dead. I urge you to get help. Here are some suggestions.

Break Out of Your Isolation

Talk to someone about your behavior and your feelings. There may be a relative or friend whom you trust. You may choose to go to a professional, such as your minister, doctor, or social agency worker.

When you stop trying to cover up and tell your story to a listening, caring person, it helps in several ways. You no longer have to bear the "big secret" alone. You gain support and guidance. You begin to have your normal needs for care and attention met by someone outside the vicious circle of abuse. You take the first step toward breaking the abuse cycle.

There may be a chapter of Parents Anonymous, or some other group of abusing parents, near you. These are parents who have either abused their children or fear that they will. You will discover that others have similar problems. You will learn new ways of parenting. You will gain emotional support for yourself.

Seek Counseling

Most abusing parents are not mentally ill. Counseling could help you by giving you better understanding of your behavior, enabling you to deal with feelings and patterns from your own personal history, and discovering ways to reduce stress and other contributing factors. You could benefit from time spent with an accepting counselor who can represent important parenting values.

A small percentage of abusing parents are mentally ill. If you are in that category, you need psychiatric help, and perhaps medication, as soon as possible. You probably recognize that in your worst moments you are not yourself. God has provided wise psychotherapists and the blessing of medication and rest to help you be your best self.

Learn More About Children and About Parenting

Expecting more from your children than they are able to perform is a major prelude to much mild and violent abuse. Children are simply not capable of some physical activities and emotional responses until they reach a certain age and stage of development. Seek a good introduction to the growth and development of children. This may be offered through your church, hospital, mental health agency, or educational institution. Pick up one of the inexpensive paperback books on child development, such as *How to Father*, by Fitzhugh Dodson, or *Child Behavior*, by Frances Ilg and Louise Ames. You will find that you relax much more, and enjoy your children more, when you realize how normal and necessary are some of their behaviors—even though they may be irritating to adults.

Broaden your ideas and attitudes about parenting. You may do this by reading some of the excellent parenting books, such as *How to Father* or *P.E.T., Parent Effectiveness Training*, by Thomas Gordon. A better way is to get into a group that is learning and sharing ideas and techniques. Again, you may find a group in your church or community agency, or you might help organize one.

Reduce Stress

What are those things which trigger your anger and abusive behavior? One of your immediate goals is to reduce stress as much as possible.

A trapped feeling may be decreased by getting a break from the children and doing something that you enjoy. Use relatives, friends, baby-sitters, child-care programs to get some regular time for yourself. Irritation can turn to full-blown hostility when you feel deprived and put upon, with no relief in sight.

Problems caused by financial stress may be hard to solve immediately. You might think of your options for improving your income and cutting expenses. Many communities have agencies that help financially troubled individuals discover ways to get back on their feet.

Dealing with the problem child is often a bigger problem when you try to handle it all by yourself. There are community agencies and professionals that are able to help you understand and relate better to a mentally retarded child, a physically handicapped child, or a hyperactive child. It is especially important in the case of a problem child to get away and have time for yourself, time to renew your energy and perspective.

In a time of illness of you or your spouse, you may call on friends, neighbors, relatives to help with some child care or other chores. This will free you to give more support to your sick mate, and have more left over to keep the family going.

Build Your Self-Esteem

A chief reason you are tempted toward child abuse is that you look to your children for companionship, affection, and care. Children are simply not capable of meeting your adult needs. Reach out to other adults, renew old friendships and make new ones. Contact family members you especially like and trust.

Realize that you are a person made in the image of God. You are one for whom Christ died. In his grace, God has already accepted you and loves you just as you are. Accept his love and live the life of one who is a very valuable person.

How to Help Others

Identify and Understand

A condemnatory approach to the abusing parent is not helpful. You will be more effective if you first get in touch with the part of yourself that is a potential abuser. You know what it is like to have "last straw" feelings. You know how frustration and anger can build until you feel like exploding. You know what it feels like to say or do something you regret later. The abusing parent will sense whether you share some degree of humanity and understanding, or whether you are approaching from a position of superiority and self-righteousness.

It is also important for you to understand that the abusing parent has enormous feelings of pain and hurt. The parent is probably already approaching zero on the self-esteem scale; child abuse adds another load of guilt and shame. Most abusing parents regret their actions but find it difficult to break out of the cycle of abuse. Your offer of friendship and understanding will help break down the walls of defensiveness.

Give Support and Friendship

Isolation is one of the major causative factors of child abuse. Parents feel unable to get their needs met for companionship, affection, and affirmation. Breaking through that isolation can relieve the pressure on family relationships to provide all that the parent needs. The parent can relieve tensions by venting feelings and talking through conflicts with you. Your attitude may help the parent feel that it is okay to make mistakes, seek information about parenting, and look for new models.

The church is an ideal institution to be of help to abusing parents. It preaches a message of grace and forgiveness and supporting love. It has many organizations and small groups which could be of help and take interest in the family. Churches usually have resources that could help teach more effective and satisfying parenting. You may be able to mobilize your church to be of help.

Provide Child Care

Your offer to provide child care may be crucial. It may be quite a relief for a parent to know that when the "last straw" comes, there is a way to step out of the situation for a while and regain composure. You may help with children during the usual times of family stress, such as moving and illness.

The resources of the church can be brought to bear on this kind of need. Many churches provide Mother's Day Out, day school for preschoolers, and after-school care. You may be able to mobilize a Sunday school class or other group to share child-care responsibilities. It will be quite satisfying for you to know that you are directly protecting this child from abuse, while at the same time giving the parent space to regroup and be a better parent.

Report Child Abuse

Most states now have laws that require the reporting of child abuse. In many states you do not have to give your name, though it helps when the child-care worker can seek more information from you. When a report is made, a child-care worker investigates to discover the facts of the situation and to offer the help of community resources. The major goal is to help the family deal with their problems and break the abuse cycle. It may be necessary in some cases to take the child out of the home for a while for the child's own safety.

I urge you to discover the resources and laws in your community, and to report child abuse when you become aware of it. It is a legal as well as a moral obligation. You may be helping a family break the abuse cycle. You may even be preventing a death.

Befriend the Abused Child

The abused child is often an isolated, lonely person. The child may feel guilt, as if he or she is to blame for all that is happening. The child may have zero self-esteem. He or she is getting constant messages: "You can't do anything right," or "I wish you had never been born." Many abused children have not learned how to play and have fun. Some are quite belligerent with other children and adults and have trouble making friends.

These characteristics have been observed in many abused children: lack of ability to enjoy and play freely, behavior problems such as aggression or avoidance, delinquent behavior, hyperactivity, low self-esteem, severe withdrawal, compulsivity, and school learning problems. You can see that the abused child is likely to be unhappy and rejected by others.

The child is unlikely to "tell" on the parents and may defend the parents if questions are asked. The child will often have confused love/hate feelings toward the abuser and will experience self-blame: "I must have done something to deserve this punishment."

It is important that you be a friend to this child. The child has the same needs as the parents—friendship, support, information, good parental models, and massive injections of self-esteem. You may help provide these individually or through church or community groups. You may be able to persuade parents to get the special help this child probably needs, such as medical attention and professional counseling.

5. Spouse Abuse

Spouse abuse is an ancient problem which has come more into public awareness in recent years. When we finally began to acknowledge child abuse and had taken faltering steps to deal with it, the way was opened to admit that spouse abuse is also a widespread problem.

BATTERED WIVES (AND HUSBANDS)

My focus in this chapter will be on violence done to women. I recognize that it also happens the other way. Men are sometimes beaten by wives or girl friends. It is difficult to tell how widespread a problem this is. The best estimates are only guesses. Abuse of women, on the other hand, has been known and sanctioned since ancient times. Women in patriarchal societies were considered the property of their husbands or fathers, much as cattle and goats were property. Women usually had no rights; their only security was to be under the care of a father, husband, or brother. If you are a physically abused man, or trying to help an abused man, read this chapter with masculine rather than feminine pronouns.

Being a Christian does not mean you are immune from spouse abuse. Your mate may have many problems that lead him to beat and otherwise mistreat you, even though you may be a faithful and devoted Christian. Some women even consider an abusive husband a cross given them by God and they put themselves through unthinkable suffering. The question I would ask you, however, is this: Does God want any of his children to go through all that?

To a world steeped in patriarchalism, Jesus preached that woman was important in her own right as a person. Divorce, for instance, was not to be based on such capricious grounds as the wife burning the morning toast, but only on the most serious grounds of infidelity (Matt. 5:32). Jesus talked with women in situations where it was considered taboo, and women became part of his group of disciples (John 4). Paul welcomed women as partners in the spreading of the gospel and wrote that among followers of Christ there is no distinction between the sexes (Acts 16:14–15; Gal. 3:28).

The good news that woman is a person and a valued child of God has not yet penetrated many segments of our culture. Many men believe that women are to have babies, keep house, and obey their husbands. Many women believe that their only security and only purpose in life is to stay with a man and meet his every need. The women's liberation movement in recent years has loudly emphasized women's rights to security, happiness, and self-fulfillment. Christians may join the effort to free women from what imprisons them, for when our Lord said, "I came that they might have life, and have it abundantly," he was including both women and men (John 10:10).

If you are locked into a situation where you are abused, what are the problems you face? What can you do about it? Why do you have such a difficult time doing anything to change the situation?

The Experience of Abuse

It seems at first unnecessary to describe to you the situation faced as an abused wife or girl friend. An abused woman surely knows what she has to contend with. Yet many women stay for years in an abusive situation, thinking that this is their place in life. It may take a long time for a woman to realize that things don't have to be this way, that, in fact, she deserves a better life as one of God's valuable children.

Have you had some of these experiences that are common to abused women?

The Violence

Problems within your spouse and problems in your marriage are expressed violently. It is hard to discuss disagreements or to work through conflicts, because you always run the risk of a violent conclusion.

You may be living with a good deal of physical pain from being slapped, hit with an object, kicked, or sexually attacked. It takes a long time for the soreness and swelling to go away, for the discoloration of bruises to subside.

It may not be the actual physical violence, but the threat of beatings or death that is such a strong club in abusing you. Whether the abuse is physical or not, the scars inside yourself, the damage to your spirit and emotions, will take a longer time to heal than the physical scars.

The Fear

You live with constant fear. When he is home, you are tight with anxiety, continually trying to read his moods, fearful that some little thing will set him off. Especially when he has been drinking, you regard him as cautiously as a ticking time bomb. When he is away from home, you are preoccupied with his coming, with his state of mind, with keeping up with a thousand details so he will have no excuse from you to explode.

Fear controls you when you think of your options. You fear that if you leave, he will hunt you down and carry out all his threats. You fear that you cannot make it on your own, economically or emotionally. You fear that he will use your leaving against you to get custody of the children.

Fear is a tyrant controlling the life of any person who keeps it on the throne. While fear will not melt away easily, it can be deposed and put in its place. Feelings of self-worth, a sense of justice, and the courage of action can push fear from an exalted position of tyranny to its rightful place as a defense signal. Most of all, the love of God can give you courage to change in spite of fear, for "perfect love casts out fear" (I John 4:18).

The Guilt

Quite likely you grew up with the strong message that it is the purpose and duty of a woman to have babies, to raise children, and, most of all, to make her husband happy. Perhaps you really believed that once you found a man and marriage, you would indeed live happily ever after.

Now things have gone sour. And you feel guilty. You have a case of the "if onlys"—if only I had kept quieter . . . if only I had cooked his favorite meal . . . if only I had raised the kids better . . . if only I were better in bed . . . The list is endless as you search your actions and personality for something you have done or some way you relate that sets off your husband.

I encourage you to think deeply about your feelings of guilt. You are responsible for your behavior, but you are not responsible for his. He must bear his own responsibility and his own guilt. Normal everyday living will bring irritations and disappointments, but does that really justify the kind of abuse you experience? Get the perspective of a trusted friend or counselor outside your family entanglements. Does that person see you taking on far more than your share of guilt and blame? Most abused women carry a heavy load of unrealistic guilt.

There may be some things about which you have real and justified guilt feelings. The Bible says that all have sinned and fall short of God's glory, and that includes you and me. If there are things you have done or left undone that you feel guilty about, the answer is confession and forgiveness. You could confess and seek forgiveness from God in prayer, with your pastor or with some trusted friend or counselor. Whatever the offense, you can be sure that the Lord will create a clean heart and renew a right spirit in you (Ps. 51:10).

What do you feel guilty about? Making a poor choice of a husband? Continuing to take abuse without doing anything to stop it? At times provoking your husband? Making excuses for him so he doesn't have to take responsibility for his own actions?

Seek out a person with whom to reflect and decide what is realistic and what is unrealistic about your guilt feelings. Confess and find forgiveness for real guilt. And let go of your unrealistic guilt feelings.

The Shame

The cloud of guilt comes when you feel you have done something wrong; shame is the embarrassed feeling that you or your marriage does not measure up. You feel ashamed that you are not a better wife and mother. You feel ashamed that your marriage is not working out. Obviously, you feel, there must be something wrong with you because the "happily ever after" has not happened.

Shame is an obstacle to your doing something to change

your situation. If you do leave and start again, you will need to tell other people what has been happening. At least now people don't know how bad it really is. You may cringe at the thought of airing your family's dirty linen before the whole world (it seems).

You will need to tell your story. You need persons who can help by their support and counsel—family members, friends, pastor, family counselor. Then you may need the help of public agencies to make a new beginning. You will find that as you tell your story in spite of the shame, you will begin to gain perspective on just how bad it has been, and on your part and his part in this. You will realize that you are not the only one who has ever experienced this; you will begin to see some alternatives. Telling your story will help you begin to overcome the shame and to make decisions about your life.

The Loneliness

One of the most painful aspects of being in an abusive family is the isolation. "Nobody comes to see us anymore."

In moods of jealousy and anger your husband has made it clear that he does not like having other people around. Even if that is not his attitude, it is difficult to maintain relationships with other people. You are not sure how or when he will explode or in some other way embarrass the family, so you and your children are very hesitant to invite friends over. You find, in fact, that when your friends get some hint of what is happening, most of them stay away.

It is difficult for your friends. They don't know how to help. They feel uncomfortable with the atmosphere of conflict and they perhaps fear for your safety. Yet they feel they have no authority to interfere in your family life. They are not aware of what measures could be taken. They may also realize, if only vaguely, the key to the situation: things will not change until you or your husband decides to change.

Those who study spouse abuse have discovered that the abused are almost always isolated persons. They suffer the jagged pain of loneliness. You can begin to overcome your isolation by picking out some person who will listen to your story and will not be frightened away, and by learning to develop friendships. You may find a family member, friend, pastor, agency worker, or fellow church member whom you can trust.

Feelings of Imprisonment

You have feelings of being in a prison because you cannot picture yourself surviving financially if you leave. You may not have job skills; even if you do, it may have been years since you had to find a position and prove yourself in a job. All kinds of other questions may arise, such as, "What will I do with the children while I work?" You may be able to take stock of your skills and resources to answer those questions; it is likely you will need the aid of a counselor or social worker to assess accurately both yourself and the job market.

Another lock on the door of your prison is emotional dependence. You may feel you cannot stand being without a man, and that any man is better than no man. Your fear of being even more alone and facing hard decisions can make it difficult to work for change in your situation.

The Good Memories

It is also hard to consider changing the situation because of the good memories you cherish. The courtship time when your husband was giving you loads of attention and vowing his undying love is difficult to give up, even if it is now only a cold memory. Thoughts of happier times you had as a couple or as a family in earlier years remain with you. Even in the roughest times of your marriage, there may be occasions when your husband is apologetic and promises to make changes. Making up after a fight may be quite satisfying and exciting.

The Fantasy

Memories of the good times help feed the fantasy that everything will change. Abused women often hold on to marriages for years with the fantasy that things will get better. You feel you can change him, you can try harder, you can turn things around. There is a principle that counselors recognize in working with human beings: a person does *not* change unless he or she *wants* to. Any lasting changes in your husband will come because he wants them. His unhappiness or his desire for something better may become so great that he will decide to behave differently. The same is true of you. When the pain of things as they are or the desire to improve them becomes great enough, you will decide to change. No one can help you change until you want to.

The Grief

In spite of the bad times, your life is meshed with your spouse in a thousand ways. You cannot live for any length of time with a person without being preoccupied with his presence and actions. It is intensified by the love you feel for him.

You may know the painful, empty feeling you get when someone close to you dies. It is similar when you consider losing your husband by separation. The grief can be even more sharply painful and more prolonged than losing by death, for the person you have "lost" is still alive.

Feelings of Worthlessness

One of the most damaged dimensions of any abused woman is her self-esteem. Because of the family you grew up in, or personal appearance, or some handicap, you may have had doubts, long before marriage about your worth as a person. Whether abuse started early or not, being abused by another person is a degrading experience. You may feel fortunate to have a man at all, even one who mistreats you.

An abused woman often blames herself for the situation. You might feel that there is something wrong with you; if you were okay and adequate, he would not mistreat you. The unrealistic standards for wives and mothers promoted by television, movies, and magazines (and some churches) could make any woman feel inadequate. You get the feeling you are not worth loving and being cared for. Most of all, you feel that you are unable to care for yourself.

The good news is that you are a Very Important Person. You are valuable in the sight of God. He has created you, blessed you with the gift of life, and considers you—along with all human beings—the crown of creation. No human being deserves what you are experiencing. I have confidence that with God's help you can stir up and use the gifts he has given you—courage, strength, and persistence. You are redeemed by the Lord Jesus Christ; you can take care of yourself and find others to care for you.

Your Self-Esteem

I want to nurture and encourage that spark of self-esteem in you. You are a child of God. You may feel like the least of God's creations; Jesus said his true friends are those who minister to "the least of these" (Matt. 25:45). Beneath whatever physical and emotional scars you have from being abused, there is a beautiful person created in the image of God. I encourage you to get in touch with that person and set her free. Build up her self-esteem as you realize you are a Very Important Person in the sight of God.

THE ALTERNATIVES

Anyone in a crisis situation has difficulty making decisions. You may be exhausted, preoccupied, fearful, confused, ambivalent. Besides all the physical and emotional drain, it is simply hard for you to see beyond the present situation and consider whether something different is possible. You have basically four choices. While you will modify your direction according to your own style, the major direction will be one of the following four.

To Stay, Unchanged

You do not have to do anything. You can stay in the situation and make no effort to change it. The result will be more years of physical and emotional battering, unless it is ended prematurely by death.

To Stay, but Change

You may choose to stay with your husband for a number of reasons but determine not to put up with abuse. You will probably need a good deal of support from family, friends, and a counseling relationship to make this work. The problem with this solution is that you can only work on changing your own behavior. If your husband is unwilling to work on changing his behavior, a happy ending is not likely.

To Leave, Unchanged

This solution has the advantage of getting you out of the situation. The beatings will stop, which is a good thing in itself. However, some of the responsibility for the situation is on your shoulders. One who does not come to understand her own past may be destined to repeat it.

To Leave and Change

A temporary or permanent separation will get you out of the situation. If you are not in the same place your spouse is, he can't hit you. Then it will be easier for you to focus on what directions you want to go with your life. You may have a clearer perspective on the possibility of your marriage being saved, on the possibility of your husband changing, and on the possibility of making it on your own. With the help of persons who care, and in time, you can make decisions based on wisdom, not on the feeling that you have no options.

How to Help Yourself

I offer the following suggestions to the woman who is tired of the status quo and ready to change it. Think about the suggestions, see how they feel to you, whether they seem to fit you and your goals in life, then decide to take some steps. Inaction will keep you exactly where you are; action is the way of hope and new direction for your life.

Call on Your Support System—Or Build One

None of us can make it through life alone. Especially when you have such big decisions and will be expending so much energy in changing, you need the supporting care of other persons. You might reach out to some understanding family members, to a few well-chosen friends, to your pastor, to your physician, to a social worker in a community agency. Whomever you select, reach out to them and tell your story; ask for care. You are not asking anyone to carry all your burdens or make all your decisions, but to stand by you and be a sounding board for your feelings and reflections. Make at least one move right away to break out of your loneliness and isolation.

An important part of a Christian's support system is God himself. He always is available to you in prayer, he always helps carry your burdens, he always cares when you are unhappy. You may feel unworthy even in God's eyes. But even if you feel far away from him, you will find that he is as close as a prayer. The psalmist spoke confidently in a time of trouble:

> God is our refuge and strength,
>   a very present help in trouble.
> Therefore we will not fear though the
>   earth should change,
>   though the mountains shake in the heart
>   of the sea.
> . . . .
> "Be still and know that I am God."
>   (Ps. 46:1–2, 10)

Discover Others with Similar Problems

You may feel that you are the only woman in the world with this burden. As you become acquainted with other abused women, you will learn that the problem is widespread. It will help to put your situation in perspective to hear what others experience. It will give you strength and hope as you hear how some have improved their situation.

Get to Safety and Refuge

Physically leaving the situation of constant violent abuse may be the only way you can survive. If things are particularly bad, there is no reason why they should improve on their own. You may find shelter with a family member or a friend, or in one of the spouse abuse centers that are springing up throughout the country.

Getting away puts you out of immediate danger. It will give you time and space to think about your future. Centers

established for abused spouses offer shelter, emotional support, referrals for legal advice, financial aid, employment and
housing guidance, medical assistance, child care, and professional counseling.

Get Counseling

At the least, you will need supportive counseling as you
face decisions and take steps to change your life. You may
also need help to discover ways you have aided in setting up
or maintaining the abusive relationship. Tragically, a woman
may finally break from an abusive husband only to find
another man who abuses her. You may need longer term
counseling to deal with those patterns of thinking and behavior which make it difficult to live the abundant life.

Begin Again . . . And Again

Whether you decide to stay with your husband and
change, or leave and change, you will need the grace to
forgive yourself again and again. You have lived a long time
with the patterns and feelings and relationships of abuse. It
is disturbing to leave what is familiar (however damaging)
and establish new ways. Of the women who decide to leave
their husbands and go on their own, only a small percentage
leave only once. Most go back one or more times with the
hope that he will change and that things will be better. If
you go back to the old situation, use it as a time of learning.
Can things really be different or are you only fooling yourself? You can see your direction more clearly when you feel
firmly about the answer to this question.

Make Your Own Decisions

You will at first turn to others for some magic solution,
for some happy ending to the whole mess. You will be

tempted to ask for advice and to follow it, instead of decid-
ing for yourself. You will not stick with the decision to
change, however, unless it becomes *your* decision. After you
have gathered advice and information, it is important that
you make your own decisions about the direction for your
life. You can do that; in fact, you are the only one who can
do that.

Take the First Step

Write down the steps you will need to take to change your
life. Put them in order of importance, from first to last.
Then take the first step to improve your life. Ask the
strength and friendship of God as you take charge of your
life as a valued child of God.

How to Help Others

There is much you can do for an abused spouse if you are
willing. It is important to be in touch with your feelings and
to be aware of the strengths and limitations of your relationship to the abused person.

Listen

Any opportunity an abused woman has to share her feelings and tell her story is important. She may not act right
away to change her situation, but just sharing will help her
overcome her isolation and loneliness. It may be the first
step in working up the courage to act.

Deal with Feelings First

You will have a natural desire when faced with a woman
undergoing abuse to get her out of the situation immediately
and help her get established in a new place. However, deal-

ing with feelings has priority over practical solutions. If feelings are not expressed and worked through, practical solutions will be brittle and temporary. It is important not to skirt the issue because of your anxiety, but to face it forthrightly and encourage open discussion. Ignoring the obvious problem only communicates that you are not able to handle the emotions of the predicament yourself.

Help Her Discover Her Resources

She may be so tense, fatigued, and preoccupied that she is unaware of her own resources. What family members or friends can she turn to? Is there a spouse abuse center nearby? Are there social agencies in the community to help? What are the laws in your state regarding the protection of adults?

Help Her Make Her Own Decisions

An important principle for most counseling is that you help the other person make his or her own decision. A decision imposed on someone you are trying to help is a dead end. If it does not work out, the woman can always blame you for your poor advice. If it does work out, the woman cannot claim fully the growth and self-confidence that comes from acting on one's own decisions. She already feels worthless and incompetent. Help her think through her situation and encourage any small decision to improve it. Your purpose is to give support and guidance but not to rescue her.

Understand

It may be hard for you to understand how a person could get into that situation, or at least why she would stay. It may be especially discouraging to help her change or leave when she soon returns. Remember the reasons why she is pulled back, the traditions and conventions that keep her there, and her overwhelming fear about facing the future alone. I have outlined earlier in this chapter some of the reasons women go back. There is often the hope (perhaps the fantasy) that things will be different.

The people who work with abused spouses sometimes get "burned out" with frustration and discouragement when they invest so much and the woman goes right back. It can be a time of learning for her, however, and you should not feel personally defeated. She will need to make her own decisions and live her own life; your responsibility is to be a faithful friend within the limits of your relationship.

Help in Concrete Ways

Perhaps you can take the children for a while, provide some transportation, find resources such as a spouse abuse center, a lawyer, or a counselor. If the woman goes to court, you can offer to go with her. Courtrooms can be frightening and confusing for any of us who are unfamiliar with them.

Spouse abuse is complex and agonizing for the victim, for the one who would help, and often for the abuser. Your concrete efforts to alleviate pressure and find resources may give the victim a sense of hope and of supportive friendship that will enable survival and change.

6. Self-Abuse in the Family

It has become increasingly clear to me in recent years that many abuses in families are rooted in the self-image of the abuser. Subtle abuses occur because the abuser feels that he or she has been denied some rights or privileges or goodies. Religious abuse hinges on the needs of the abusing individual or institution for survival or power or self-righteousness. Child abuse and spouse abuse are often perpetuated by persons with zero self-esteem who feel deeply threatened by the least slight or rejection.

Often when persons are abused in families, the result of the incident is injury to the abuser. A beaten child will eventually show great hostility toward the parent, or become a broken-spirited individual who never becomes a fully grown adult. Neither outcome is satisfying for the abuser. An abused wife may knuckle under, but she will never give the kind of love and companionship that makes for a satisfying and rewarding marriage. The result of even the subtle abuses is not the abundant life, but a life of dissatisfaction, tension, and self-centeredness.

Most abuses in families seem outwardly to be directed toward the abused person. However, some examples make it clear that often the abuser is getting defeat and destruction as a payoff. An abusive, alcoholic man begs his wife to give him one more chance. She does, and three days later he comes home drunk, beats her again, and she leaves for good. It is as if he intends to create as miserable and lonely an existence as possible. A woman constantly accuses her husband of having affairs, though there is no evidence or apparent motivation except her fear that she will lose him. She puts all her energy into searching for evidence and nagging him. He finally feels he can no longer live with a woman who offers only suspicion and nagging, and leaves. What she fears has happened—and it has confirmed her feeling that she is not worthy of another's love and deserves rejection.

The most flagrant self-abuse is suicide. There may be motives related to family members, but the suicide victim suffers most. There is no changing of that decision once the act is successful. Suicide is the ultimate self-abuse, the crown of feelings of unworthiness and low self-esteem. This does affect the family, of course, and the ripples from suicide may never be finally stilled. The family is abused by the loss of the person, by feelings of guilt (realistic or unrealistic), by shame that this has happened in the family, by the haunting fear that another family member may commit the same act. But the suicide victim has the biggest loss—life itself.

Why Self-Defeating and Suicidal Behavior?

Self-defeating behavior may be seen on a scale. At the bottom of the scale are minor obstacles to self-fulfillment. At the top of the scale is the ultimate self-defeat, suicide. It is all self-defeating and self-abusing, and it has in common some basic causes. You may find some roots of your self-abusing behavior in this list.

Low Self-Esteem

You are probably plagued with a chronic feeling of unworthiness. Somehow it seems that you can never measure up. As you look around, it seems that everybody else is smarter, stronger, more skillful, more talented, better-looking, better clothed— The list could go on and on.

You may have gotten some messages from your parents that you are inadequate and in some way do not measure up. You have not reexamined and left behind those childhood feelings of incompetence that we all have. There was a time when you could not walk or talk or tie your shoes; you may be hanging on to the inadequacy feelings rather than to the feelings of achievement that came when you were successful and accomplished developmental goals.

Not only do you feel inferior to others, you feel unworthy. You are reluctant to take the time of another person. You feel eternally grateful that some "important" person may pay attention to you. You feel you are wasting the time of any person in authority—teacher, pastor, community leader —who stops to talk with you.

Your attitude toward yourself is the sin of not thinking of yourself as highly as you ought. God made persons "a little lower than the angels" (Ps. 8:5), but you are behaving as if you are lower than a snake's belly in a wagon rut. You are not respecting the image of God that is in you as well as every other human being. You are not seeing yourself as a redeemed child of God.

Self-Hatred

A step beyond low self-esteem is self-hatred. Not only do you feel yourself inferior and unworthy but you begin to despise your appearance, your voice, your actions. Not only are you unworthy of the attention of other persons but you actually deserve to be mistreated, hurt, and beaten down. The extreme of this is the person who seeks physical beatings as a curious way of finding satisfaction. You need not go that far, for there are many ways to set it up so you are continually frustrated, feel unloved, and suffer abuse and failure.

Again, you are denying the image of God in you and the death of Christ on your behalf. You need forgiveness for treating one of God's creations (yourself) so poorly. You need counseling help to correct your attitude toward yourself.

Revenge

Revenge is behind much self-destructive behavior. A relatively mild form of family abuse, withholding, may have revenge as its motive. The elder brother in the biblical story of the prodigal son was angry with his father and his younger brother. He felt slighted. He felt he had not been rewarded for his faithfulness (did he envy the "riotous living" of his younger brother?), and was jealous of the outward display of affection toward the returned young man. He expressed his anger by withholding his presence (and blessing) from the homecoming dinner. Jesus makes it clear that the elder brother was the biggest loser. His air of superiority and withholding kept him from a full, satisfying relationship with his father and brother. Indeed, it made him a symbol of the scribes and Pharisees, who were called whitewashed tombs by Jesus.

You may feel that your behavior is making your family members suffer, when it turns out that you suffer most of all.

The ultimate self-defeat, suicide, may have revenge as its motive. "I'll show them; they'll be sorry." Writers of suicide notes often assume they will be around afterward to see the sorrow and remorse of family members—even if they do not believe in a life after death. You may say, "I will be around, for I believe in life after death." But do you think heaven will be the kind of place where Christians will look down in glee on the sufferings of those left behind? The revenge motive for suicide does not make logical sense.

Desire for revenge and punishment of those responsible for real or imagined grievances is self-defeating. It eats away at you like an untreated cancer which gradually destroys all your vitality.

Feelings of Powerlessness

When persons feel trapped and powerless, violence may erupt. Some social movements of our century have been tinged with violence. When workingmen felt put down by employers, trapped in an economic ghetto, and powerless to change conditions, their frustration was expressed violently. One significant root of the ghetto riots in the 1960's was found to be a prevailing feeling of powerlessness.

Violence is a way of affirming oneself when one feels powerless and helpless to change an unbearable situation. Abusing a child or beating a spouse may be your way of affirming that at least you have power over someone. It is a way of making someone recognize your existence and your control. Suicide may be a final desperate act to affirm that you exist, or that you are important. You may have a picture in your mind of your family grieving and being full of remorse at your funeral. You may feel that you will get much more attention in death than in life.

The trouble is that you will not be around to get the attention. Your violence to a family member or to yourself will only make things worse for you. Violence is a sign of weakness and of inability to get your needs met in other ways. You need help to find more constructive and satisfying behavior that will result in confidence, hope, and a sense of personal strength.

Hopelessness

Closely related to the feeling of powerlessness is an outlook of hopelessness. You have the feeling that nothing can change, that the future will be just as dismal as the present.

A small town in a northeastern state was to be covered by the water behind a new dam. The dam was needed to produce electricity, and the lake over the town would be a recreation center. When this news became public, all maintenance and upkeep work in the town ceased. No one wanted to put money and effort into buildings that had no future. Months before the dam was completed, the town had become a run-down, dilapidated shadow of its former self.

When the future seems bleak, there is no energy or enthusiasm for the present. In your hopeless state you may be abusing family members out of a sense of frustration and depression. You may be abusing yourself by procrastination or letting your body, mind, and spirit become dilapidated. You may be giving up your sense of rightness and wrongness —if there is no worthwhile future, you may say to yourself why be ethical? You may be considering suicide to end the frustration and boredom.

The writer of the book of Proverbs is right: "Where there is no vision, the people perish" (Prov. 29:18). Where there is no hope for the future, the days are dry and dusty. Boredom and despair set in.

You can overcome your feelings of despair and hopelessness if you get in touch with the hope we have in Jesus

Christ. In the worst of circumstances, we have hope for new beginnings and for the coming of God's Kingdom.

Stress

Stress is necessary to some degree to keep us energized and motivated. However, you might find yourself subject to massive amounts of stress. The words "overburdened" or "burned out" may describe your feelings. You arrive at the "last straw" stage where you feel that you just cannot face another problem. Your external stresses have built up internal pressure, and you feel ready to blow a fuse.

One answer to stress is reevaluation of your priorities. What situation or situations are causing you the most stress? Something at work? Your finances? Family conflict? Significant personal losses you are grieving over? What can you change about those things? Can you renegotiate some relationships or tasks? Can you free yourself from some situations that are not really valuable to you? You may be putting up with some pressures which could be eliminated. You get confused and your perspective is blurred when you are overstressed. You are important enough to find some ways to give yourself relief from external and internal pressures.

Avoidance

Self-defeating and suicidal behavior may be seen as avoidance. When you abuse your child or your spouse, you are avoiding the hard work of parenting or marriage-building. You may be avoiding grief by abuse—grief over a lost child, spouse, parent, or dream. In your efforts to avoid grieving, you may channel your anger destructively toward your family or yourself.

Your behavior may be designed to avoid the risk of rejection. You are not tender with your spouse because you fear misunderstanding and rejection. You avoid the scariness of taking a chance in personal relationships. Your attitude is, I'm going to be misunderstood and rejected anyway; I might as well be what I'm expected to be.

A suicide attempt is the ultimate avoidance. If you succeed, you successfully avoid responsibility for yourself and others and the possibility of rejection. Suicide is not the act of a strong person. It is the action of a person who feels too weak to contend any longer with the ambiguities of life.

THE ANTIDOTE TO SELF-ABUSE

Self-abuse is a poison destroying every facet of your life. I have a prescription for you. The antidote to self-abuse is Christian faith, love, and hope. You can have your Christian perspective awakened and learn more fully what the Christian life and faith is. You can know that God loves you and that you can love yourself. Your life can have meaning. You can live with hope.

God Loves You

The whole point of the creation story of Genesis is that God made man and woman to be his companions. We are in his image. We have freedom, creativity, and authority over the rest of creation. We have the potential to love. You are part of the crown of God's creation.

The point of the life, death, and resurrection of Christ was to redeem human beings. We have strayed, we have sinned, we have fallen short of the glory of God. He has done his redemptive work in Christ so that each person— including you—could become a full child of his. The picture of God presented by Jesus is that of the seeking shepherd who does not rest until the least of the sheep is safe in the fold (Matt. 18:12–14). It is the picture of the loving father welcoming home the prodigal son (Luke 15:22–24).

"Consider the lilies of the field . . ." God creates and cares for flowers and birds in a marvelous way, and you are much more valuable to him than any of these (Matt. 6:26–30).

God loves you and likes you. If you despise yourself, you are putting yourself on the other side of the fence from God.

God provides for you in times of fear. He loves you when you are hurt and rejected. He provides a way out when burdens seem unbearable. He will give you the gift of his presence in the hardest of times. His presence with you brings strength and peace and a sense of joy.

To be loved by God, you will have to give up acting as if *you* are God. You do not have control over all of life. You cannot force other persons to be or to act just as you would wish. You cannot spare yourself all disappointments and rough times. But you can acknowledge God's power and give him direction in your life. Isaiah speaks to those who feel forgotten by God and describes his sustaining care:

> Why do you say, O Jacob,
>   and speak, O Israel,
> "My way is hid from the LORD,
>   and my right is disregarded by my God"?
> Have you not known? Have you not heard?
> The LORD is the everlasting God,
>   the Creator of the ends of the earth.
> He does not faint or grow weary,
>   his understanding is unsearchable.
> He gives power to the faint,
>   and to him who has no might he increases
>   strength.
> Even youths shall faint and be weary,
>   and young men shall fall exhausted;

but they who wait for the LORD shall renew
    their strength,
they shall mount up with wings like eagles,
they shall run and not be weary,
    they shall walk and not faint.
                                        (Isa. 40:27–31)

You Can Love Yourself

A false notion has crept into Christianity, the notion that
to be human is to be a lowly, despicable creature. "Such a
worm as I" is a theme of Christians who feel themselves to
be so far short of the glory of God that they disparage
everything human.

How dare we despise the crown of God's creation! In an
effort to discourage selfishness, the proper love of self has
been overlooked.

The goal of the Christian is not to be perfect—that would
be to eat of the forbidden fruit, to try to be God ourselves.
The goal is to be fully human. Your aim as a Christian is to
become all that God intended when he created humanity.
My son recently was given a novelty Frisbee on which is
printed: "Christians aren't perfect, just forgiven." You can
be all that God has intended. Even as you stumble and fall
at times, God has provided prayer, confession, and forgiveness for you.

When Jesus was asked what is the greatest commandment, he said it has two parts: love God with your whole
being, and love your neighbor as yourself. He assumed that
persons love themselves. His illustration of neighbor-love is
the story of the good Samaritan. It teaches that the neighbor is anyone in need who calls for responsive care and
concern and action. To know what proper self-love is, picture yourself as the victim of robbery and beating on the
Jericho road. You are just as worthy as the man in the

story of being cared for and having your wounds bound. And you may be in the best position to be a good Samaritan to your wounded, bleeding self! That is proper self-love —to give yourself the quality of care you would give to anyone else.

Self-contempt leads to self-abuse. It keeps you from appreciating and valuing yourself as you are. When you truly value yourself, you want the best in life. You want to lay up for yourself treasures—treasures that will not rust or become moth-eaten, but lasting treasures. This means that you will avoid those "pleasures" which seem so attractive at first but will eventually tear you down and destroy you. When you love yourself properly, you will not want to abuse yourself with excessive alcohol, drug addiction, promiscuity, or irresponsible job behavior.

You will value yourself more than money, education, power, or fashion. Many persons value their possessions rather than their essential selves. Like the rich young ruler, they go sadly away from the presence of God because externals have such a great hold on them. The rich young ruler did not love himself well enough to give up wealth and power and take the eternal life that Jesus offered (Mark 10:17–22).

You are not a god; neither are you a mere animal. You are tempted to think of yourself more highly than you ought, and perhaps to control all facets of your life and your family members. You are also tempted to think of yourself as the lowest worm. But you have freedom, responsibility, and the potential for creativity and love. God himself has blessed your humanity by becoming a human being like you: "the Word became flesh." Jesus Christ offers forgiveness and redemption and new beginning. Paul says the Christian goal is to attain "mature manhood, to the measure of the stature of the fulness of Christ" (Eph. 4:13). You can love yourself with the kind of love that spills over as appreciation, respect, and wanting the "abundant life."

Seek a Community

Self-abuse is the behavior of a very lonely person. Even if you are surrounded by a crowd of people wherever you turn, you are not forming relationships that enable you to have your needs met and enjoy life. Paul wisely observes, "None of us lives to himself, and none of us dies to himself" (Rom. 14:7). Not only do we need God, we need the blessing of other persons.

Your family may be the place to find this. Take a look at them and your relationship to them. Is there potential for strong, satisfying relationships? Can there be forgiveness and healing? Can you and your family, perhaps with outside help, become more of what God intends you to be?

Is there a Christian fellowship you may join (or rejoin)? Though churches are not always what they ought to be, I have seen many redeemed, healing, caring fellowships of Christians. The potential is there for all the members to function as one body, with Christ as its head and love as the glue that holds it together. Community is at the heart of the Christian faith. In both the Old and the New Testament, there is no individual salvation. To become a child of God is always to become a part of the people of God.

One question you will have to ask yourself in relation to your family or a Christian fellowship is: Will I allow myself to be loved? Will I open my life to others and give them a chance to appreciate and care for me? Will I find a group with whom I can share those inexpressible secrets? These problems will lose their power over you when they are shared with someone you trust.

You can be helped with your stress in a community of

Christians, for we are admonished to bear one another's burdens. The person who cares for you does not take all your load and treat you like a weak child. That person stoops down, gets under the load with you, and strains with you in partnership.

Your Life Can Have Meaning

Your self-abuse may be related to a lack of meaning in your life. If you have no vision larger than the constricted world of your own personal problems, your life feels empty. There seems to be no reason to live. A psychiatrist in a World War II concentration camp noticed that some of his fellow prisoners would fold and die under the constant stress and heavy work load. Others stayed alive through terrible, degrading experiences. The only difference he could detect was that the persons who lived had some purpose in their lives. Sometimes as a hospital minister I will ask a patient who is in particularly grueling circumstances, "What keeps you going?" Some patients mention family members. Some talk of the support and love they experience from God.

You can have the strength that comes from purposeful living. Family members or work or recreation activities may help give your life meaning. Along with these, God offers you a place in the most worthwhile project possible, the building of the Kingdom of God. As you envision taking your place with the host of those who are committed to him, and working and loving and ministering in his service, you can be part of a purpose that is infinitely beyond individual problems and purposes. Purposeful living for the sake of God can energize your life and give it excitement.

The Christian Hope

The antidote for self-contempt and self-abuse is Christian faith, love, and hope. But I would not mislead you. As a Christian, you will not be spared pain and suffering and rejection. This is an imperfect world where injustice and unfairness and misery sometimes have the upper hand. In Christian faith you see unblinkingly the realities of the world, but you also experience hope.

No matter how bad your circumstances are, there is hope. You can hope for a better future. You can hope the sour aspects of your life will change. Family abusers and self-abusers can and do change their behavior. Even those who would destroy themselves find that suicidal impulses are temporary; they will pass with time and effort. Most of all, you can confidently hope for the presence and blessing of God in your future. There can be power and joy in your present, for there is hope in your future.

My hopes for you are blue skies, high self-esteem, strong family relationships, and meaningful living. But I know that neither you nor I will always have that. There will be times when life is not easy. Yet the Christian faith promises joy even in the worst of times. "More than that, we rejoice in our sufferings, knowing that suffering produces endurance, and endurance produces character, and character produces hope, and hope does not disappoint us, because God's love has been poured into our hearts through the Holy Spirit which has been given to us" (Rom. 5:3–5).

HOW TO HELP YOURSELF

Seek Counseling

Look for a professional person with whom you can establish a counseling relationship. This may be your pastor, a social worker, a psychologist, a psychiatrist, a mental health agency worker. You need to break out of your loneliness and isolation and allow someone else to know what is going on with you. You need to know why you set yourself up for failure. You need to understand why you have self-contempt. You may need to make some new decisions about yourself.

You especially need immediate help if you have been preoccupied with suicidal thoughts. You need help right away to strengthen your lifeline. Moving into counseling can be a move of hope and growth.

Relieve Stress

Take a look at the stresses that pressure you. What sort of stress do you experience at work, with your family, in other areas of your life? What is the level of your internal pressure? How much conflict do you have within yourself that cannot be easily resolved?

Make some decisions about your stress points. There may be some relationships and commitments that you can renegotiate. There may be other relationships and commitments that need to be jettisoned so that the ship of your life will stay afloat. Reexamine your priorities. Your physical, mental, and spiritual health should be very high on your list of priorities.

Love Yourself

Self-love and selfishness are not the same. Selfishness results when you focus only on yourself and use others for your gain. Proper self-love is having appreciation and respect for yourself. It is wanting the best for yourself and acting to take care of yourself. You cannot properly love your neighbor until you have appropriate self-regard. Seek those treasures in life which will be ultimately rewarding and satisfying and upbuilding for your life.

Have Patience

Your low self-esteem and self-abusive behavior need not be permanent. Even if you feel self-destructive right now, it is a temporary attitude. Give yourself time to rebuild your respect for yourself. Give yourself time to discover the roots of your discontent and to appropriate the gifts of the Spirit of God. If you follow your impulses and self-destruct, there will be no later opportunity to change your decision.

Claim the Peace and Power of the Christian Faith

God has promised us many blessings in the Scriptures. We describe these blessings with words like "salvation," "redemption," "forgiveness," "eternal life." What it means for you right now is that God will be closer to you than any friend can be. He will strengthen you and give you peace and patience. He will give you meaning in your life. He will give you bright hope for the future. You are a very important person to God! Put your life in his hands and enjoy the blessings of his care.

How to Help Others

Build Self-Esteem

Whether the self-abuse you see in another person is subtle and mild, or tends toward suicide, that person needs to be affirmed and supported. You can be of help by giving respect and admiration wherever possible. Do all you can to increase realistically that person's self-esteem. That person needs to know that someone else in the world considers him or her important.

Offer Friendship

The person with self-contempt usually feels unworthy of the love and attention of others. This may be true even when the abusive person acts quite aloof and arrogant. Your offer of friendship says that you consider the self-abusive person to be worthy of your attention and time. You may be in the best position to serve as a bridge between the suicidal person and help. Your encouragement may make the difference.

Take Suicidal Talk and Gestures Seriously

There is a myth that persons who talk about suicide or make suicidal gestures are not really intent on destroying themselves. This is not true. Most of the persons who have committed suicide have given signals to other people several times before the successful act. Even though a suicidal gesture may be "only to get attention," the person may accidentally succeed. Suicidal thoughts and actions should be taken seriously.

Get Help

Become acquainted with the resources in your community that are available to help self-destructive and suicidal persons. It would help you to know where the emergency intake centers are for suicidal persons. It will be helpful also to know resources for counseling and therapy from medical, pastoral, and social service personnel.

You may be able to refer a person to a resource for counseling in the community. You may be part of an effort to get a self-destructive person committed to a facility until the danger is past. In any case, assure the suicidal person that, whatever help he or she gets, you will stand by as a friend and be available to support and to care during and after the treatment process.

Exercise Your Christian Faith

It may be appropriate at some point with a self-destructive person to share your faith and hope in Christ. If so, a simple statement of how God helps you through hard times and a reassurance of God's love for that other person are very important. If you do not have an appropriate opportunity to testify verbally to your faith, you can still give an important witness by your attitudes and actions of trust, hope, and love. The person in distress will understand the message of your attitudes and actions far better than any sermon you could preach. And you can pray for healing and help for the abuser.

Those who work in suicide prevention centers are advised to look for one significant person in the life of the potential suicide victim. That person could be an important tie between life and death. Acting in the spirit of the good Shepherd who left the ninety-nine in the safe fold and went out to find the one lost and in need of help, you could be that one helpful person.

Epilogue
Hope for Family Abusers

The bad news is that all of us engage in family abuse, whether it is mild and subtle or obvious and severe. Just when we think we are immune, the words of Paul confront us: "Therefore let any one who thinks that he stands take heed lest he fall. No temptation has overtaken you that is not common to man" (I Cor. 10:12–13). The potential for the most destructive action is present in each of us.

The good news comes to us also through Paul's words: "God is faithful, and he will not let you be tempted beyond your strength, but with the temptation he will also provide the way of escape, that you may be able to endure it" (I Cor. 10:13). While Paul recognizes that each of us may be overtaken by temptation, he is quick to add that God provides avenues of escape and endurance.

There are times when we might escape temptation to abuse through changing our geographical location immediately—walking into the next room or getting a baby-sitter and going out. Escape may come through wholesome activities, times with friends, conversation on a crisis hotline, or counseling for new perspectives. Escape may come in prayer as we seek the wisdom of God. Endurance is available to us through prayer, Christian fellowship, and all the resources of God's people.

The bad news becomes good news as God enables us to rekindle that deep love and desire to care for those closest to us.

For Further Reading

Dodson, Fitzhugh. *How to Father.* New American Library, 1975.

Duvall, Evelyn Millis. *Faith in Families.* Abingdon Press, 1970.

Gordon, Thomas A. *P.E.T., Parent Effectiveness Training.* New American Library, 1975.

Hudson, R. Lofton. *Helping Each Other Be Human.* Word Books, 1970.

Irwin, Theodore. *To Combat Child Abuse and Neglect.* Public Affairs Pamphlets, 1974.

Justice, Rita, and Justice, Blair. *The Abusing Family.* Human Sciences Press, 1976.

Kempe, Ruth S., and Kempe, C. Henry. *Child Abuse.* Harvard University Press, 1978.

Roy, Maria, ed. *Battered Women: A Psychosocial Study of Domestic Violence.* Van Nostrand Reinhold Co., 1977.

Organizations That Help

Abused Women's Aid in Crisis, Inc. (AWAIC), G.P.O. Box 1699 New York, N.Y. 10001.
A clearinghouse for information and referral.

National Center for the Prevention and Treatment of Child Abuse and Neglect. University of Colorado Medical Center, 1001 Jasmine Street, Denver, Colo. 80220.
A clearinghouse for information and materials.

Parents Anonymous, Inc., 2810 Artesia Boulevard, Redondo Beach, Calif. 90278.
For information on PA groups.

Your local mental health agency and crisis hotline.

Your local church.